1951 Beadle coach

EAST KENT Explored

Best wishes -
Nick Evans

by NICK EVANS

Published independently

First published in 2005 by Nick Evans, Whitstable, Kent CT5 1RT

A catalogue record for this book is available from the British Library

ISBN 0-9545252-1-3

Printed and bound in Great Britain by Thanet Press Ltd, Margate, Kent

By the same author: Dreamland Remembered – 140 years of seaside fun in Margate ISBN 09545252-0-5
Charting the story of Margate's famous amusement park as well as the Lido, Cliftonville.

Front cover illustration: Taken from a 1920s travel poster showing a charabanc on the quayside at Sandwich.

Contents

Introduction

SOON after the arrival of the internal combustion engine followed the omnibus, bringing a cheaper and more flexible form of mass transport.

It's now 100 years since the first boneshaker buses trundled around the roads of south east England and for the past 90, the foremost name has been that of East Kent.

Smaller than its regional neighbours, East Kent more than held its own through good times and bad. It was born out of a war and took a full part in a second. It survived the nadir of nationalisation and has thrived again since privatisation.

East Kent Explored takes an affectionate look at this company and some of the people who have worked for it over the years. Judging by the numbers who stayed for 25, 30 or even 40 years, it can't have been too bad an organisation to work for!

The book aims to give the reader a local history perspective of the company and the area it continues to serve – just consider the East Kent buildings which have been redeveloped in fairly recent times – but there is plenty for the bus enthusiast to enjoy.

There must be many who remember summer outings to the coast on one of East Kent's express coaches while others will recall trips on an open top bus. Evenings out would begin and end with a bus ride, long before widespread car ownership took hold.

Of course, buses are there for more than the fun things in life, getting us to and from school, work or the shops. East Kent buses have knitted themselves into the social fabric of life in this area of England and no doubt will continue to do so as we try to avoid total gridlock on our busy roads.

I'm indebted to a number of people and organisations who have helped produce this book by allowing me to plunder their collections of photographs and memorabilia and gladly record my warmest thanks, in particular to Brian Weeden and Nicholas King of the Maidstone & District and East Kent Bus Club for their advice and assistance. A full list of contributors can be found at the back of the book.

There are many thousands of images of East Kent vehicles so the ones chosen here can only be a representative sample. I hope you will agree that it is an impressive collection, acting as a fine record of past times.

Nick Evans
Whitstable
August 2005

1. East Kent Road Car Company's first headquarters building in Station Road West, Canterbury.

Born out of necessity

IT was born out of necessity as the war to end all wars raged only 100 miles away from them.

It was while thc British Army continued to take heavy losses on the Somme in France that chiefs of the five larger bus companies around east Kent agreed it was vital to pool their resources if they were to stay in business.

The birth wasn't an easy one as negotiations dragged on for some months but finally a deal was struck and the East Kent Road Car Company officially came into being on 11 August 1916.

Ever since the First World War had begun exactly two years earlier there had been growing shortages of fuel, spare parts, vehicles and crews to put buses on the road as men and resources were diverted to fight the Bosch.

Sidney Garcke, an early private motorist and head of Deal & District Motor Services, called and chaired a meeting in Canterbury of the various local owners in April 1916. Sidney, then aged 31, was the son of Emile Garcke, founder of the British Electric Traction (BET) Group.

He was joined by Frederick Wacher of Wacher & Co of Herne Bay; Walter French of Thanet based Margate, Canterbury and District; George Griggs of Ramsgate Motor Coaches at Dumpton; and Walter Wolsey, manager of Folkestone District, a subsidiary of the substantial Thomas Tilling company.

The legalities of transferring the assets of the five firms into the new company were addressed and on 18 July 1916 an Extraordinary General Meeting gave the go ahead.

East Kent Road Car Company began trading on 1 September. The name of the fledgling operation had its detractors during the negotiations. Walter Wolsey had long admired the London Road Car Company and considered the term 'Road Car' to reflect tradition. The terms 'Traction' would have been the choice of Garcke and 'Motor Services' by French.

The five directors met for the first time as a board five days after East Kent's formation in the Canterbury offices of solicitors Mowll & Mowll in Castle Street. Chairman was Sidney Garcke who had lost little time appointing Alfred Baynton, William Norton and TG Chadburn respectively as secretary, traffic manager and chief engineer. The company itself would

become an associate of the fast growing BET organisation.

Although mainly taken up with legal duties, other decisions were agreed including that the company's livery would be mainly red and bear the East Kent name on both sides of the vehicle. The first to wear the new colours was a Deal and District Daimler single decker which had been resprayed by a garage in Ringwould.

Wartime restrictions continued to bite. Later in 1916 it was decided that no complete uniforms would be issued to staff until conditions eased – but drivers were given oilskins while conductors did get hats and overcoats.

Formation had given East Kent a mixed collection of 72 vehicles with premises at Deal, Canterbury, Folkestone and Margate. There were a dozen different makes in the fleet but by the end of the year only 40 vehicles were in running order. Somehow they managed to carry 4.5 million fare paying passengers at this time, employing 200 people.

2. An East Kent clippie of 1916. Women took the place of men called for war duty.

3. All aboard this ex Folkestone District Tilling-Stevens built charabanc of 1914 with a later 1922 body.

4. Fuel rationing in the First World War forced East Kent to adapt buses to run on gas. The gas would be carried in a bag on the roof and here one vehicle calls in for a top up at Canterbury gas works.

Vehicles in these far off days tended to be ponderous, noisy and unreliable. Solid tyres were still widely used and the wheels themselves made of wood. These would shrink in dry weather and would have fallen to pieces but for the fact they were taken off the bus every night and soaked in water!

The noise factor became too much to bear for the Vicar of one Cheriton church who wrote to the company complaining about East Kent's noisy buses and requested they should not pass his church between 6.30pm and 8pm when Sunday evensong was being held.

At a meeting of one council there was long discussion over whether the buses were ventilated too much or too little. The Medical Officer stated: "The atmosphere was appalling in a red bus on a dirty day."

One councillor argued there was really too much ventilation as passengers were sometimes almost blown out of their seats.

Until 1931 buses were not able to take to the roads without consent and licensing by local authorities and certainly the councils in east Kent were keen to ensure their wishes were followed – and charged accordingly.

An emergency provisions act of 1916 forbade new routes for buses without the agreement of all the highway bodies affected. Kent County Council acting for itself and district bodies decreed that bus proprietors must pay the greater of £10 per route mile per year, or 1d per bus mile for waterbound roads, 0.75 of a penny per bus mile for tarmac roads and three eighths of a penny per mile for roads with concrete foundations. Lack of consistent licensing would dog East Kent for a number of years after hostilities ceased but gradually authorities took a slightly more pragmatic approach.

Towards the end of 1917 and during 1918 supplies of petrol were strictly rationed and were only obtainable on permits. To mitigate the effects of rationing, a number of vehicles were adapted to run on coal gas. The gas was carried in a collapsible bag on the roof.

This necessitated ensuring trees were regularly lopped along routes – much to the annoyance of residents and councils – but on one day in 1917 two of the fragile bags were blown off buses while serving coastal roads at Capel between Folkestone and Dover. The bags were blown out to sea and never seen again – perhaps they were mistaken as a new secret weapon by enemy eyes!

Shoppers and passengers who could choose their own times of travel were asked to avoid peak hours so that work people could be successfully conveyed. At night times passengers were discouraged from paying their fares with paper money as conductors couldn't easily distinguish values in light restricted conditions.

Permits were also required to enter Dover – extensively fortified at this time and a major Naval base – with a complete ban on journeys leaving or arriving in the town after 8pm. Enemy aircraft and Zeppelins were making regular raids in 1917 and bombarded the town no less than 18 times.

In Folkestone, Shorncliffe Barracks had become a major embarkation base for soldiers bound for France. Buses would be full to bursting as these men boarded, anxious for one more fling before facing life in the trenches. Military personnel were asked to keep order as the men got on the buses and also helped collect fares when alighting.

Six months after the end of the First World War, conditions had improved sufficiently for the company to resume its Canterbury to Dover route in April 1919. As that year drew to a close other main roads were also seeing services return but it would still be a long time before the East Kent network was complete.

Competition was certainly intense and at one time on the Dover to Folkestone route there were as many as 18 departures in 20 minutes.

Much of this extra competition came from men returning from war with gratuities and buying one or two charabancs to operate themselves. This happened all over east Kent but quiet winters saw them absorbed or disappear. Between 1917 and 1935 more than 50 smaller operators were bought out by the company.

In early 1917, with most towns in southern England being served by one or other of East Kent, Maidstone & District or Southdown buses, it became a priority to reach an agreement to define each company's boundaries. By the spring, East Kent's borders were fixed on a line east of Faversham, via Ashford to Rye and Hastings. This would prove to be an area which would stay largely unchanged for more than half a century.

5. East Kent's entry in the Herne Bay carnival of 1919 depicted the past, present and future of public transport. The horse and cart represented the past, a Daimler bus the present, and a biplane on a lorry for the future.

6. Crowds of spectators gathered to cheer buses as they returned stranded holidaymakers to London after a rail strike in1919 left hundreds in the area without any means of getting home. Here, passengers board in Herne Bay.

East Kent unwittingly operated its first express coach services in September 1919 when a sudden railway strike left hundreds of holidaymakers stranded in the coastal towns. The company quickly put together services from Folkestone, Deal, Thanet and Herne Bay to London to get these people home. Fares from Folkestone were £1 for the five hour long single journey or, if you needed to come back, 30 shillings (£1.50) for the return fare. The services caused a sensation with

7. Early days in Deal captured outside the Beach Hotel (now The Royal) in 1920. The group includes a number of the local staff pictured with a Daimler B bus of 1915 vintage originally belonging to Margate, Canterbury & District.

spectators cheering the departing buses!

It was the experience gained from this rescue mission which paved the way for scheduled express services to be introduced between east Kent and London in spring 1921.

In May of that year East Kent partnered with fellow British Electric Traction (BET) subsidiary Motor Coaches of London to operate a London to Margate service. Vehicles would set out from their own terminals and exchange passengers at Maidstone – or in the event of delay, where the vehicles met. This must have been mildly discomforting for passengers to say the least!

The 1920s would prove to be a decade of slow but steady progress, new routes being developed and existing ones being consolidated in the face of competition – or competitors being bought out.

As services to London became daily occurrences during the following 12 months, so East Kent was able to influence the development of Victoria Coach Station, a terminal still used extensively by operators from around Britain.

The seaside towns of Margate, Broadstairs and Ramsgate proved a difficult nut to crack for several years. Here, East Kent was up against the Isle of Thanet Electricity Supply Company's tramway running from Westbrook via Margate to Ramsgate as well as its own bus network for the parts not covered by tram. The tramway owners also supplied electricity to the area so it's perhaps not surprising the licensing authority run by the local councils was pretty strict towards outside competition. The situation only eased once local operators were acquired later on in the decade to boost East Kent's modest number of 10 vehicles already present on the isle.

Further round the coast, the port of Dover offered the company two more challenges. Here again was an established municipal tramway while the town's steep hills put a damper on building new housing. Any suggestions by Sidney Garcke for joint operations around the town centre met with resistance for several years. However, there was a breakthrough in 1923 when East Kent built a new garage there.

8. The inaugural run of the Folkestone to Canterbury service in March 1919. Driver and conductor have stopped in the centre of Elham, the halfway point, in their Tilling-Stevens single decker recently acquired for this service.

9. A Tilling-Stevens TS3AX with Palmer built bodywork poses at Margate Harbour in 1921. The vehicle stayed in the fleet until 1930 when it was sold on.

The seemingly more affluent towns of Folkestone and Hythe were eyed up with enthusiasm by the company management. The area was a boon to holidaymakers – seen as far more sedate than Margate or Ramsgate to the north – and retained military strongholds at Shorncliffe and Hythe as well as a busy port at Folkestone.

Competition on this stretch of coast was particularly fierce but routes serving Shorncliffe, Cheriton, Wood Avenue, Folkestone Harbour and Sandgate to Hythe would prove to be East Kent's most profitable until close to the outbreak of the second world war.

Just how competitive the routes were is revealed in this reminiscence by a conductor published later an issue of the East Kent staff magazine: "We had a bad day. The takings were poor. Arrived in the garage about 10.30pm. The Old Man asked Charlie how were things today? Charlie replied: What d'yer expect with a fool like that behind the steering wheel? He knows nothing about bussin' and strikes me he never will. All he thinks about is gettin' 'is gears nice and being perlite to everybody. 'E says it isn't right to keep to the middle of the road to 'old the opposition back. I don't want 'im no more!"

Other routes, some covering long distances, were put in place to operate between Rye and Hastings while a through route from Margate to Hastings, running via Folkestone and New Romney, was started in 1921. Future developments in east Sussex were boosted by acquisitions, most notably that of Wright & Pankhurst at Rye in 1930.

10. The conductress posing by her bus in the 1920s gives a good indication of how large were the vehicles. Lucy Chittenden served nearly 40 years with East Kent.

Ashford was initially a low priority for route development by East Kent. The town's status as a centre of the Southern Railway's works meant its large number of employees and their families were given generous travel discounts – on the trains. By 1927 though East Kent believed town services here would be viable and opened its first depot in Station Road.

East Kent's fare charging structure was simple enough during the early 1920s. Everyone, whether adult or child, paid the same single journey price but by 1925 the first return fares were introduced on a few routes and an adult could carry a child under three for free. Half fares for children aged between three and 14 would follow some years later but only where the adult single was more than threepence.

The company claimed to be the first in the country to introduce season tickets for its regular travellers in 1926 and within the first 12 months 1,400 had been issued. At this time weekly 'Anywhere' weekly tickets could also be obtained for 25 shillings (£1.25 in today's money) during the off season rising to 30 shillings (£1.50) for the summer months but peaking at 40 shillings (£2) in August and early September.

A service which would last for many years, even until the days of nationalisation, did not involve carrying passengers but transporting parcels. In August 1928 a scheme was introduced enabling packages weighing up to 50lbs (just over 20 kilos) to be handed in at any of the company's network of offices or 30 specially appointed agents.

Parcels could also be given to a conductor on the bus itself. Charges were based on single fares over a range weights and a 4lb package would be carried in 1929 for just 4d (2p).

New housing was appearing on the outskirts of several towns in east Kent during the 1920s and their development saw the arrival of a number of new short run, high frequency town services. February 1927 saw three new routes in Canterbury alone, serving Whitstable Road to Old Dover Road, London Road to St Martin's Hill and Wincheap to Sturry Road.

11. A view of East Kent's bus station at St Peter's Place, Canterbury, captured probably in 1923. In 1956 it was superseded by the St George's bus station which was itself redeveloped in 2001.

12. This Daimler bus was one of a batch of more than 40 to arrive with East Kent in 1920. It was given a new body by Shorts of Rochester in 1927 and stayed in the fleet until 1933.

13. Right, a period drawing of one of East Kent's buses driving through the narrow archway of Canterbury's West Gate – taken from a message card posted in 1926.

It was soon discovered that the cost of carrying a conductor on these routes made the difference between profit and loss. Not wanting to lose money, management came up with a special collecting box in which the three halfpence fare would be paid. Coins were passed into two glass guides attached to the box. The driver, having checked the right money was offered, then released the coins into the box. No tickets were issued and the cash was collected later in the day by a superintendent.

Initially 14 seater Morris vehicles were used around the city but as popularity grew, larger 20 seater Tilling-Stevens buses, specially rebodied with front entrances, took over duties.

East Kent's first purpose built double decker buses made their debut in 1927. These were three reconditioned Daimler Y type chassis on to which open topped bodies by Straker had been mounted. The bodies had been purchased from London General which had itself acquired them second hand.

East Kent's experiments with the double deckers proved successful and orders for new vehicles were placed over the next couple of years with Leyland for chassis and open top, open staircased bodies by Short Brothers of Rochester. These lasted a number of years, despite falling from grace by the late 1930s when covered top double deckers were holding sway. After rebodying, some saw service beyond the end of the war.

Southern Railway became a significant shareholder in East Kent from 1928 owing to new powers to operate road services and two of its nominees were appointed to the company board. Before long SR's holding in the company built up to 49 per cent. This move saw tickets becoming interchangeable on some routes – passengers who had travelled by coach from London to the area could return on the train if they wished for payment of a small supplement, for example.

Such a large holding in East Kent also paved the way, it is argued by many railway enthusiasts, for the closure to passengers of the Canterbury to Whitstable line, fondly known as the Crab & Winkle, in December 1930.

14. Front cover of one of a series of local guides published for East Kent during the late 1920s. It discusses the future growth of the local coalfield.

15. It's unusual to see a charabanc with its hood up – and can only have meant misery for its occupants. New in 1926, this Tilling-Stevens was later rebodied and was withdrawn in 1936. It had a new lease of life with a travelling fair.

16. This single decker was one of a batch of 43 delivered in 1929 designed to carry 37 passengers. The chassis was supplied by Tilling-Stevens and the body by Shorts. It stayed in the fleet until 1938.

Closing the Crab &Winkle caused consternation in the area and a delegation of Canterbury traders visited the management of Southern Railway at Waterloo to be reminded of its shareholding. An SR traffic manager told them passenger numbers on the line had more than halved in the previous five years and it could not continue to lose money.

"If the public prefer buses, they can have them," he told the traders. "Southern Railway is now one of the biggest shareholders in the East Kent Road Car Company so what we lose on the swings we gain on the roundabouts."

As the 1920s came to a close, East Kent was in a strong financial position with an average balance of £54,000 for the three financial years to September 1930. Aside from its fleet of buses and coaches, now serving an extensive network, it had property assets as well. A new garage was built at St Stephen's in Canterbury during 1925, Russell Street, Dover, had been occupied since 1923 while in Thanet there were several small sites including a coachworks in Dane Road, Margate. The site for Westwood depot had been acquired in 1927 and after opening in 1931 it would be the company's largest such site. A small garage was acquired at the Horsebridge in Whitstable on takeover from Wood Brothers of Blean in 1927.

In 1929 an arrangement was agreed with the Post Office where letter boxes would be installed in some buses. This enabled people living in rural areas to post mail up to an hour later in the day than they could otherwise. The buses involved carried a board declaring Post Car in red letters.

Mail was already being carried by East Kent from rural areas to larger towns where it would be collected by Post Office messenger and taken to the local sorting office.

The new decade heralded a sweeping change in the way services were licensed and operated. The 1930 Road Traffic Act set up separate and independent Traffic Commissioners who were given the task of licensing vehicles, drivers, conductors and services as well as approving fare increases and timetabling.

Despite some initial confusion as the new legislation came into effect, things settled down and would influence the entire British bus industry for the next 50 years or so.

From the outset the benefits to East Kent quickly became obvious. Instead of having to deal with 22 different licensing bodies in its area, it now only had to deal with one. The act also increased the maximum speed of buses to 30mph and saw the first control of drivers' hours.

On the flip side of the coin, Britain was now beset by economic depression and profits fell markedly to less than £30,000 a year in the early 1930s. Amid rising unemployment and cutbacks, seaside holidays were low on the list of priorities and to a company which relied heavily on summer trade this spelled disaster. Redundancies among staff followed with service reductions.

The company weathered the storm and managed to replace no less than 170 of its oldest vehicles – some dating from the First World War era – bringing greater standardisation to the fleet. Orders included more double deckers which had, at last, been given approval to operate in the Canterbury and Folkestone areas after a number of refusals by the local councils.

There had been alarm in some quarters when the company announced its plans to introduce double deckers. The objections, to the modern mind, are laughable. One vicar complained simply because he did not like the look of them while others drew an hysterical picture of ceilings falling down and foundations being shaken in houses. Another objection was there would be no privacy for residents as passengers travelling up top could peer through bedroom windows. A suggestion that a higher fare should be charged for this additional entertainment did not meet with universal approval!

As East Kent marked its 20th anniversary in 1936 it operated 540 vehicles and was carrying 28 million passengers and expected to reach 30 million before long. It put its growth down

17. Standing at Margate Harbour is one of East Kent's first purpose built double deckers. A Leyland TS1 with bodywork by Shorts of Rochester, it was delivered in 1930 and survived after rebodying as a single decker until 1949.

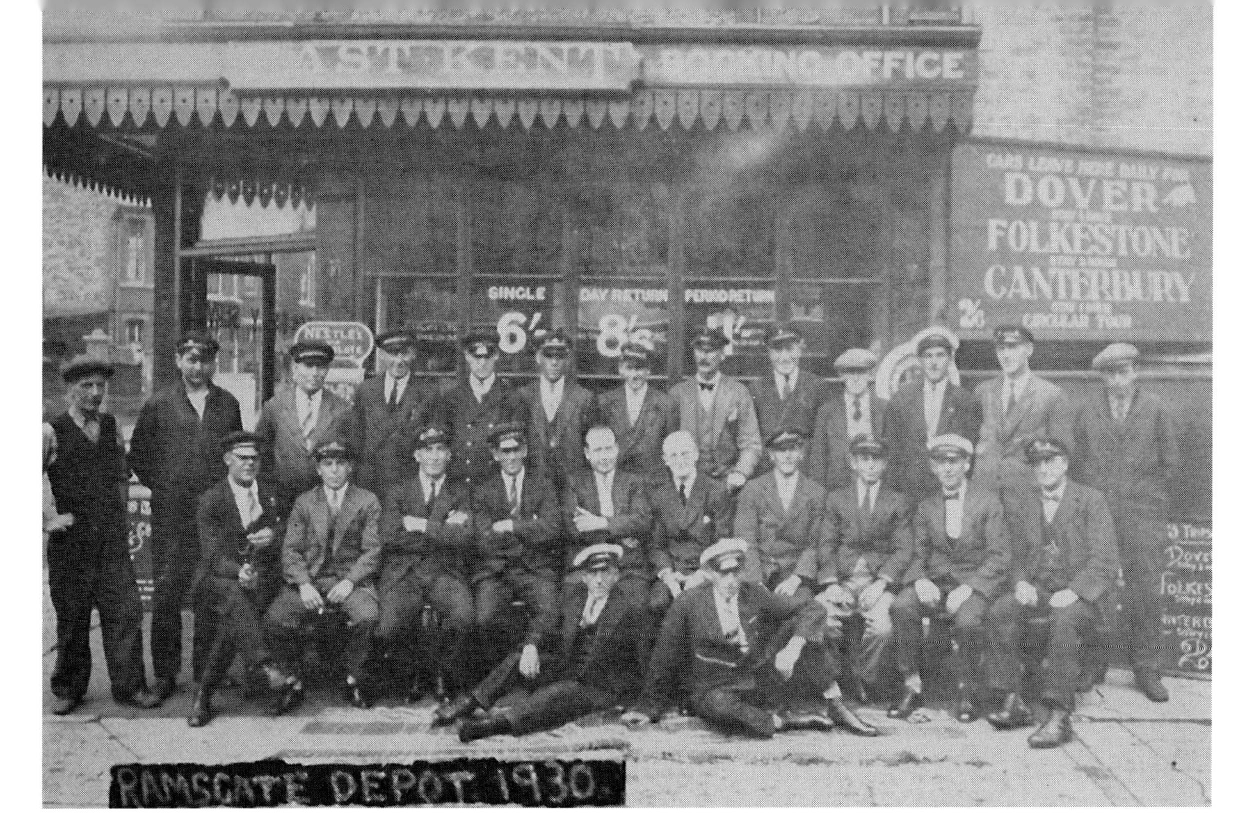

18. East Kent staff were often commended for their courtesy and politeness – always important to create a good impression for holidaymakers. This group of 'gentlemen of the road' at the Ramsgate booking office dates from 1930.

partly to a combination of smoother roads, pneumatic tyres, springing, braking and more efficient engines.

East Kent employed around 1,300 people and its staff were renowned for their courtesy and politeness – sometimes being referred to as 'gentlemen of the road'. The management was also happy, and no doubt relieved, to note that during its first 20 years nobody had been killed while travelling on the buses!

19. Leaflets advertising drives in the countryside with East Kent. Summer excursions were enjoyed by many in the late 1930s on the company's comfortable coaches. They were an important part of the business for many years.

20. Children – and further back, some of the staff – get set for an eagerly anticipated summer outing aboard at least three 35 seater Dennis Lancet buses. That in the foreground was new in 1936 and lasted until 1950.

Most notable among the takeovers of the 1930s were the tramway systems in Dover and Thanet.

Dover's municipal tramway dated from 1897, making it the first in southern England. East Kent expressed an interest in buying it out in April 1934 and after the council had appointed an adviser – the general manager of Birmingham Corporation Transport – a deal was struck for the trams to be replaced by buses from 1 January 1937.

The agreement insisted that all of East Kent's takings in the town area were pooled and 75 per cent of the profits were paid to Dover Corporation after expenses and a 3d per mile capitation charge.

21. Leyland Titan double deckers were introduced to replace trams in Margate and Dover in 1937. Fifty were purchased for the work, 29 being based in Thanet with the remainder sent to Dover. A trio of Titans waits at Margate.

22. Chestfield Golf Club, near Whitstable, provides the backdrop for a 1939 Dennis Lancet bus with Park Royal body. This was one of a number of vehicles to have a well recessed into the roof to enable band instruments to be carried. The photo was taken just after the Second World War.

The tram depot at Buckland was rented to the company for £112 per year and although not used for some time, proved its worth when Russell Street was severely bomb damaged in 1942.

Dover's trams, replaced by a fleet of mainly Leyland TD4 double deckers, met an inglorious end. Enclosed vehicles were sold off to scrap metal contractors but the open toppers were driven out to River and burnt.

The Isle of Thanet Electric Tramway had been created in 1901 and had bought its first motor buses in 1912 to supplement services where trams did not run.

Margate Corporation, aware of claims that domestic electricity supply services provided by the company were subsidising the trams, set up a transport committee in August 1933 to keep an eye on the situation.

Two years later the three councils of Margate, Broadstairs and Ramsgate appointed a consultant to determine if there was a future for the network. Evidently, there wasn't and by May 1936 it was agreed to abandon the trams by the following March. In August 1936 a shareholders'

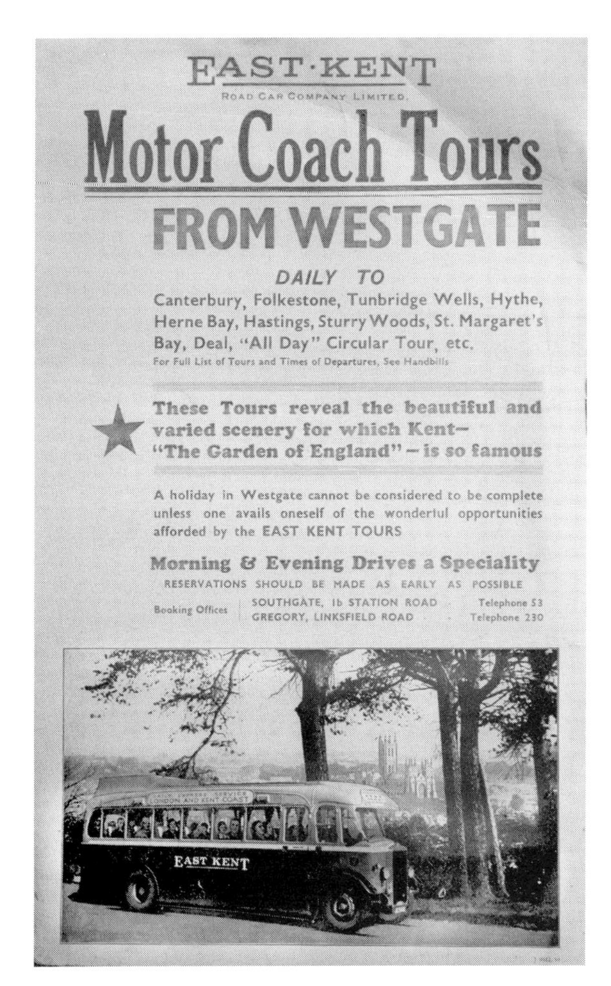

23. A holiday in the small Thanet seaside town of Westgate simply wasn't complete without an East Kent coach tour according to this 1938 poster.

24. Express coach services between east Kent and London were a popular means of travel – and about one third less than the standard third class rail ticket. Perhaps this vehicle provided the model for that in the advertisement below.

25. Visitors to Whitstable during the 1930s could expect to see this advertisement for East Kent services included with a local street map.

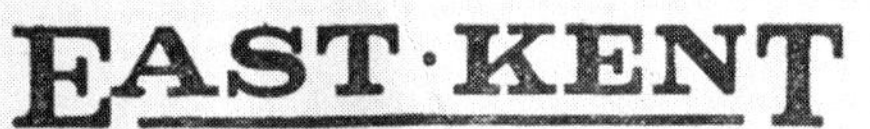

ROAD CAR COMPANY LIMITED.

Operate Daily Time-Tabled

ROAD CAR SERVICES

FROM WHITSTABLE

to Canterbury, Herne Bay, Faversham and Margate, with connections to all parts of East Kent.

LONDON-WHITSTABLE SERVICE DAILY

Well appointed Motor Coaches make daily excursions during the season to all places of interest.

Luxurious Coaches for Private Hire.

Apply for Time-Tables (2d. each) and full particulars to the local Company's office :—

HORSE BRIDGE, WHITSTABLE

Telephone : WHITSTABLE 294.

meeting agreed to sell the entire operation to East Kent for £135,000, including its buses.

After running the operation for a few months on an agency basis, the company properly took over from 25 March 1937.

East Kent inherited 49 buses comprising 11 Thorneycroft and 30 Daimler single deckers as well as nine Daimler double deckers, two of which were open top. Those that weren't sold or scrapped lived on to be repainted in the new owner's colours.

Among these were five double deckers which had only arrived the year before. They had Daimler COG5 chassis with five cylinder Gardner engines, flywheel transmission and preselect gearboxes with bodies built by Weymann. They stayed in use until 1950 operating around Thanet, Canterbury and Herne Bay having survived a variety of wartime experiences.

The trams themselves were scrapped at St Peter's depot which also passed into East Kent ownership.

At this time the company employed around 400 drivers and conductors across the area, most of whom were taken on for the summer period when traffic was at its busiest and most profitable.

East Kent, largely because of its geography, relied heavily on summer trade and those of 1938 and 1939 were particularly good, each breaking previous records. This success also meant it was able to invest in a total of more than 60 new vehicles, largely Leyland TD5s with Park Royal or Brush 53 seat lowbridge bodies. But it was as summer 1939 was coming to an end that this rosy picture changed virtually overnight.

26. Air raid practice as children rush off their bus to a nearby shelter in St Peter's Place, Canterbury. This was one of a series of photos taken for propaganda. The same vehicle AJG 5 was used in all of them.

Fighting for the Home Front

THOUSANDS of children being evacuated to Kent from London was a sure sign that war was on its way.

Some 8,000 arrived shortly after German troops had invaded Poland on 1 September 1939. Youngsters were met by a fleet of East Kent buses ready to take them to a wide area taking in Canterbury, Hythe, Chartham, Sturry and Lyminge. Many more children were taken to other towns but the majority had returned to the capital by Christmas. Not long after, the buses were involved again evacuating children away from east Kent to what were deemed to be safer parts of the country.

The declaration of war itself quickly meant much of the company's trade disappeared – holidaymakers were soon homeward bound while many residents made arrangements to live elsewhere if they could.

Authorities lost little time in rationing fuel and before the end of September East Kent's services had been halved while a maximum speed of 20mph had been imposed for all vehicles travelling in built up areas.

In the event of an air raid bus crews were instructed to drive to the nearest shelter and wait there until the all clear had sounded.

Blackout was strictly enforced at night causing more headaches for crews. As well as there being no street lighting, headlights were masked to prevent both detection from above and lighting the way ahead for an enemy to follow. Buildings were left in darkness and of course all direction signs and obvious landmarks had been taken down too.

From a murky exterior, it wasn't much better on board as only dim blue light bulbs were permitted inside, with stairs and platform

27. Standing by a shelter in Dover, a 1936 built Leyland TD4 gets set to leave on route 87 bound for Ramsgate via Whitfield, Eastry and Sandwich during the 1940s. Note the wartime livery where grey replaced cream paintwork.

entirely unlit. The only ways of knowing a bus was coming was to hear it or chance to see the white painted edges of its front wings!

Also during September, following an arrangement made with the Ministry of Health some months before, 30 Leyland TS7 coaches were converted for use as ambulances, each being equipped with stretchers.

They were manned 24 hours a day in the event of major air strike and distributed between garages at Herne Bay, Canterbury and Ashford. During the hostilities that would follow, the numbers of ambulance coaches varied and by early 1945 there were 14 left. Owing to their

28. Some of the Leyland TS7 coaches which were equipped as ambulances to be used by the civil defence in the event of major air raids. This group of vehicles formed part of the allocation to Ashford depot.

comparatively low mileages by then, East Kent would be able to convert them back to coaches and kept them in the fleet until the mid 1950s.

The end of the Phoney War – that early period of hostilities which saw no air raids or major attacks on Britain – heralded what was arguably East Kent's finest hour, its contribution to the evacuation of the British army from Dunkerque.

At 4am on 27 May the company received telephoned instructions to have 250 vehicles and drivers ready for urgent use. In less than three hours it was proud to be able to report that buses and crews were standing by. They had actually been brought together at a central point between Ashford and Canterbury before dispersal to Margate, Ramsgate, Folkestone and Dover with 50 of these held in reserve in Canterbury.

Instructions were simple: "Send all the vehicles you can, first coaches, then single decks and lastly double deckers."

Air attacks were expected at any moment and returning soldiers were to be transferred from the ports to railheads with minimum delay. Operations lasted for several days, the drivers willingly working day and night, stopping only to snatch brief meals and sleep. They were joined in the task by clerks, foremen and fitters who would take buses out whenever they could be spared.

29. Thanks to its proximity to occupied France, Dover was repeatedly bombed and shelled throughout the war. Here, East Kent staff prepare their sign boards announcing route changes in the area when attacks were expected.

★

Sandwich Salute the Soldier Week

APRIL 29th to MAY 6th

Fred used to drive a bus on the Dover Road; Bert was a Conductor known to many thousands on a Thanet Route; Bill was a fitter in the Works—they epitomise the many of our employees who are serving in the British Army in all theatres of war. We salute them this week and look to their early and victorious return to their peace-time occupation. Let us speed their return by an increase in our weekly savings so that they shall lack none of the essentials necessary to beat the Hun.

EAST·KENT
ROAD CAR COMPANY LIMITED.

30. Newspaper advert promoting the Sandwich Salute the Soldier Week – year unknown – to boost war savings.

Adding to this logistical challenge was a shortage of railway rolling stock which led to some buses going on longer than intended journeys – 30 being sent to Redhill and 40 to Chatham on one day.

The hard work put in by the busmen at that crucial time is largely unrecorded – certainly there were no official records kept by the company – but, in its way, must rank alongside that of the flotilla of Little Ships which plucked the same troops from the Dunkerque beaches themselves.

Kent now came into the front line, the coastal towns were evacuated and changed from being a reception area to becoming one of defence, ready to bear the brunt of a likely invasion.

Residence and movement in the area was strictly limited and generally a pass was required to get into or out of the coastal towns. To use a camera was to risk arrest and detention.

In the early days after Dunkerque, vehicles were hired with drivers and and attached to Army units to replace transport lost in France. Some 55 buses and their vehicles spent six months in the Suffolk countryside, looked after by a small maintenance squad whose mobile workshop was a 1.5 ton lorry, their service pit was a trench in the corner of a field lined with planks and strutted with tree trunks.

Business was again at a low ebb so to produce much needed revenue spare vehicles were hired to other operators, some as far away as Scotland. By the end of 1941 some 122 vehicles had been hired out to fellow BET Federation companies and other operators. In some cases the buses were repainted into the hirer's livery, as with Aldershot & District and Southdown. The latter went so far as fitting its own liveried radiators as well. Companies were charged £2 per day per bus on top of all running expenses paid for by the hirer.

East Kent buses were sent out on long term hire to the Midlands to carry workers to armaments factories and to the Army moving troops around the countryside. This included one notable occasion when anti-aircraft gun crews were transported at a moment's notice from Dover to Purfleet in Essex to minimise the Luftwaffe's attacks on the London Docks. Forming part of an escorted convoy, it was a weary group of drivers who returned home after a long day and night away.

By mid 1940 nearly 50 East Kent buses had been sent to the Kidderminster area to transport workers to factories or labourers to help rebuild them after bombing. Again, service pits were built in fields and there was a constant battle for spare parts to keep the wheels turning.

Madam will you walk?

That is a risk you take if you wait for the last bus, for if everyone did so, it couldn't carry all who wished to travel.

The last bus is an emergency service to carry passengers who have been unexpectedly delayed. In these times, extra buses cannot be run to accommodate tardy travellers.

So do not plan to travel by the last bus; catch an earlier one; leave the last bus for those who through force of circumstances must rely upon it to get them to their destination.

CVS-14

31. One of a series of newspaper adverts placed by the company urging people to not to take up valuable seats on buses.

While engine changes could be carried out at Midland Red's local depot, buses in need of major repairs were sent back to Canterbury. On at least three occasions, vehicles were driven on to low loader rail wagons and their tyres deflated to ensure they would pass safely under bridges.

By taking on additional contracts towards Derby and Leicester – and later on at Lincoln – some 80 buses were involved when the work peaked in 1943. By the end of that year though the number of buses had fallen to 28 and by the end of 1944 virtually all had made their homeward bound journey.

Closer to home the picture was grim. Luftwaffe aircraft had been attacking the area for some time – one of the first German bombs to fall on Britain destroyed East Kent's small office at The Horsebridge in Whitstable on 13 August 1940 – but people were determined to take a business as usual approach if they could.

32. Gas producer trailers were fitted to a number of buses in 1943 to save precious fuel. The trailers were inefficient, only being able to produce half the power required for a bus. They gradually disappeared as fuel supplies increased again.

33. The Whitstable office at The Horsebridge took a direct hit in August 1940, completely destroying the building. Bookings and parcels operations were continued via agents in the town. An arts centre now stands on the site.

34. AJG 5, new in 1938, continues its propaganda tour visiting a debris strewn Dover. The idea of showing life continuing as normal would have been more plausible if the rear destination blind hadn't shown a Canterbury route!

Buses were an easy target for lone strafing enemy aircraft as they wended their way around east Kent's largely flat open countryside. The cream coloured parts of vehicle paintwork meant buses could easily be seen from the air so were repainted grey. Combined with bombing raids and cross Channel shelling, particularly on Dover, it's little wonder this difficult time became known as the 'Busman's Malta' reminiscent of the heavy pounding that island was taking at the time.

Crews were not bound to stay in the south eastern part of the county if they did not wish to as the company offered to pay for their evacuation away from the front line. It was their own choice to endure bombing, shelling and run the risk of being shot at without means of retaliation. The steep winding road out of Dover – the predecessor of the Jubilee Way – was described by East Kent's traffic manager as 'the loneliest road in England'. It was only the buses which dared to climb the hill and on clear days the enemy would have a good view of their movements from the other side of the Channel.

In the best traditions of wanting to do their bit for the war effort, staff were formed into a specialist Home Guard unit. Each depot had its own platoon with the intention of defending their site in the event of invasion. Later, the role changed to help provide a mobile force taking other Home Guards around the county to where they might be needed most.

The 45 or so drivers working in the Midlands were not left out either. In fact, they became particularly good shots as they were able to get plenty of rifle practice with scarce ammunition 'donated' by a local arms factory.

As the war progressed most of East Kent's garages were damaged one way or another – some of them direct hits – and dozens of vehicles were lost as a result.

Still in Dover, the Russell Street garage became a regular target but on 23 April 1942 the most tragic of incidents happened. A bomb made a direct impact on the air raid shelter in which 10 members of staff were taking cover. Nine died either instantly or later in hospital. The tenth man survived after being trapped for one and half hours and later returned after the war for a long career with the company. In the same raid an inspector was killed when his office in Market Square was hit.

There was heavy damage to buses, the garage and offices, forcing a move to the old Buckland tram depot to continue operations as best as possible.

35. All aboard Ada for a welcome cup of tea. ADU 470, a 1934 Daimler, became a mobile canteen in Dover.

Later in the war as the D-Day invasion got under way, the bus terminus was moved to Pencester Road. The temporary encampment saw two former Isle of Thanet Daimler buses respectively become a mobile office and canteen. The latter thanks to its registration of ADU 470, was known to all as Ada. This bus went on to become a tree lopper in later years, remaining in use until 1958 when it was sold.

The town's Home Guard lent its field kitchen while crews slept under canvas but at least a special permit was granted to give them extra food rations.

Canterbury also was a frequent target for visiting Germans and St Stephen's garage was an early war casualty at the height of the Battle of Britain in September 1940. It took a direct hit, badly damaging a number of buses and buildings. A valuable stock of tyres – already in short supply – and £500 worth of bus tickets were also lost.

36. The garage in Russell Street, Dover, was attacked several times – most notably in 1942.

37. Another picture for the propagandists, this time by St George's Church in Canterbury city centre. Note the fuel tanker carrying pool petrol.

The Baedekker raid of 31 May 1942 over the city brought worse news. The garage and body repair works were completely rased to the ground as was company headquarters in Station Road West, just around the corner. Eight buses were totally destroyed and another 33 seriously damaged. Luckily, there were no human casualties. Repairs began within 24 hours at Faversham depot but much of the company's records and office equipment were damaged beyond repair.

A week or so later traffic and engineering staff were housed in Alcroft Grange, Tyler Hill, on the

38. Alcroft Grange at Tyler Hill on the city outskirts, became the temporary home for East Kent staff. People were taken there by a Leyland TS7 coach and TD5 double decker.

39. St Peter's depot near Broadstairs was badly damaged by enemy action in 1943. The former Thanet tram depot remained operational and was later used for winter storage of surplus vehicles. These days it is an industrial estate.

40. St Stephen's garage, Canterbury, in 1943 showing an open top Leyland Titan then used for hop and fruit picking work, a Daimler, a Tilling-Stevens single decker and two Leyland Titans. To the right is a wartime Guy utility bus.

41. Their sign says it all. Women drivers and conductors of Canterbury depot gathered for a group photo in 1943. Some of the ladies were still working for the company 25 years or so later.

northern edge of the city. The general manager moved to Tunbridge Wells but secretaries had been moved sometime before in late 1940 to the Robin Hood Cafe at Charing on the A20.

At the end of October 1942 two tragedies on the same day, close together on the Canterbury to Herne Bay route, deeply affected staff.

One Canterbury bound Daimler was attacked as it approached Calcott Hill near Sturry. Sparks were seen flying from the road by the conductress, a new employee who had only joined a few days before. Assuming there was something wrong with the bus she frantically signalled the driver to stop. At that moment the vehicle left the road and ploughed into a field and she then saw the unmistakable outline of a German fighter which continued firing on the stricken vehicle. Eventually, the conductress managed to help the passengers escape but the driver was not so lucky. A bullet had killed him

42. This time it's the turn of the Deal ladies for a team picture and, again, a few were still with East Kent well into the 1960s. Many of the men would have been away fighting in the armed forces when the picture was taken.

43. St Peter's bus station in Canterbury during the war. The vehicle on the left belongs to Maidstone & District.

at the wheel, passing through the back of his seat, and had been deflected up into the roof. A cannon shell had blown off part of the radiator.

The second bus was attacked as it left the city with a bomb landing on the rear of the vehicle, killing the conductress and nine passengers. The driver was cut about the head by broken glass but, with help, quickly got survivors off the bus. The courage of the staff at this time is exemplified in a report which stated that 'another bus was sent out for them'. Despite the fact the German raider was still thought to be nearby, a replacement vehicle left without hesitation to pick up survivors.

The St Peter's depot near Broadstairs was badly affected by blast damage in another raid during the summer of 1943. Garage, stores and workshops there were stricken, fire watchers at the time saying the sole German plane passed so close as it dropped its two bombs they could see raindrops bouncing off the wings.

By 1943, the war had been taking its toll for four years. The need for new vehicles in the fleet was a pressing one – as the last to be delivered had been back in 1940. The Ministry of Supply had drawn up specifications for standard double and single deck vehicles which could be built with minimum skills and costs. The utility bus had arrived.

Use of aluminium was prohibited, making for a weight increase in the new design of about

The Long and Short of it

Don't take a long-distance bus for a short journey —you may crowd out someone who wants to travel all the way. The number of long-distance buses is limited, and based on careful examination of the needs of the districts served; a missed long-distance bus may mean a long wait for the next one.

So use the local buses for local journeys and leave the long-distance buses for long distance passengers.

44. Another newspaper advertisement imploring people to travel wisely on the services available.

45. By September 1944 East Kent had taken delivery of this line of 10 Guy utility specification buses. Bodies for this batch were by Park Royal.

20 per cent, while seats were made of hard wooden slats instead of moquette fabric. All chassis were to be made by Guy of Wolverhampton, the Ministry decreed, based on the pre-war Arab and came with either Gardner 5LW or 6LW engines. Bodies were made by many major builders. Very often a batch of buses being delivered to an operator would have a slight variation in body styles but all would meet the rigid war time specifications.

East Kent fared quite well in this scheme and all of its Guy Arab utility vehicles had their preferred Park Royal or Weymann bodies. The first three arrived in the area in early 1943 with another 20 by the end of 1944. Things were beginning to look up in 1945 as the last 50 or so utility buses were fitted with upholstered seats once more. It's worth noting here that no single deckers or coaches were supplied new to East Kent after 1940.

The D-Day invasion of 1944 brought an end to long range shelling and bus spotting sorties by the Luftwaffe but the threats posed by V1 and V2 flying bombs meant caution was still required. As the war finally ended, the job of rebuilding the company, against a continuing background of shortages and hardship, became the top priority.

Code for Blackout

1. Keep off the road — use the footpath.
2. Signal a bus with something white, such as a newspaper.
3. Don't flash a torch in the driver's face, it may cause a serious accident. If you *do* signal with a torch, shine it on the ground at your feet.
4. Don't step out to meet an approaching bus — the driver can't see you.
5. Don't jump on or off a moving bus.
6. Keep your mind on the traffic and don't be a jay-walker.

EAST·KENT
ROAD CAR COMPANY LIMITED.

CVS-16

46. Instructions on how to summon a bus during the blackout were vital for public safety.

47. Leyland PS1 coach CFN 60 was one of only four new vehicles to be delivered to East Kent in 1946. Here, it turns out of North Lane, Canterbury, as an ex Isle of Thanet double decker rounds the nearby West Gate Tower.

Rebuilding and regeneration

ALTHOUGH peace had returned to Europe in May 1945 wartime restrictions would persist for some years after, frustrating British industry's attempts to quickly recover from the war.

East Kent had lost a total of 132 single deck buses and coaches through military requisition or destruction but, thanks to deliveries of replacement utility buses, it had 38 more double deckers in 1945 than in 1939 for a total fleet of 441.

Replacing a depleted and worn out collection of vehicles, rebuilding bomb damaged offices and garages or overcoming shortages of fuel and spare parts brought plenty of challenges for the management.

All of these vital components and many more needed for efficient recovery were carefully controlled by a government licensing scheme to ensure that

48. Two East Kent buses collided with one another, overturning this Leyland TD4, at Priest & Sow Corner, Whitstable, in 1946 injuring 14 people. The other vehicle involved was a Dennis single decker.

49. Leyland PD1 CJG 986, new in 1947, stops in New Romney High Street on its way to the Army camp at Lydd in 1959.

highest priorities were met first. East Kent lost little time placing orders for new vehicles when it received the appropriate licences in September 1945. Fifty Leyland PS1 coaches and 60 Dennis Lancet single decker buses, all with Park Royal bodies, were required. The first ones did not arrive until October 1946 – when only four were handed over – and February 1947 respectively. Others would trickle through slowly and the order would not be completed until 1948 and 1949.

Leyland received an order from East Kent in

50. East Kent ordered 72 Dennis Lancets – all with Park Royal bodies – including CFN 134 which is arriving in Hastings from Rye. It would be rebuilt in 1959 for one man operation.

51. JG 9928, with its 1948 ECW body work, stands at Reculver on the frequent service from Herne Bay towards the end of its life in 1962.

September 1946 for 50 PD1A Titan double decker chassis, with Leyland bodies, and these were eventually delivered from October 1947 until January 1948, the last being a PD2.

Arrival of these vehicles finally allowed the oldest in the fleet to be retired after many years service. It also enabled 24 pre war Leyland double deckers to be sent to Lowestoft in 1948 for rebodying by Eastern Coach Works as lowbridge 55 seaters. The following year 35 more went to London's Park Royal works, again to re-emerge as lowbridge vehicles. Putting new bodies on to older chassis became common practice in several fleets and helped keep numbers up to strength. In fact the last of these two batches would see service until 1963.

Probably the most notable example of getting extra life out of older vehicles surrounds the conversion by Beadles of Dartford of pre war engine and chassis units into an integral body structure. Known as the Beadle Rebuild, the idea caught on among several BET operators and from East Kent saw a total of 28 Leyland TD5

52. The new St Stephen's garage, Canterbury, on which work was completed in 1948. A Dennis Lancet, converted for one man operation, rests at the front.

53. One of the Beadle Rebuilds, GFN 259, pauses at the Central Hotel, Gillingham, for a refreshment stop en route to Herne Bay and Whitstable. Its roof boat rack was fitted in 1963.

chassis returning with full front, forward entrance 35 seat coaches. These facelifted vehicles led useful lives and some carried on until the mid 1960s.

Odsal House in Harbledown, on the outskirts of Canterbury, was acquired in January 1946 as temporary headquarters, bringing back together the admin departments which had been spread around the county during hostilities. Rebuilding went ahead at St Stephen's garage in the centre of Canterbury to allow the body and paint shops to return from Faversham and Margate. A shortage of cement held up work though and prevented completion until 1948.

Despite living amid shortages and austerity, people were determined to have some fun in this era of demob suits and gratuities. There had been no chance for leisure and holidays during wartime so many were keen to make up for lost time.

New cars were in short supply too and many people would have to make do with older models. That meant travelling any distance was still the preserve of trains and coaches.

54. The South Coast Express service was jointly operated by East Kent, M&D, Southdown and Royal Blue.

Passengers taking their first chance in years to get away for a few days ensured good express coach business for East Kent. Services from Victoria Coach Station in London resumed in late February 1946 – making the company one of the first to do so. The news was tempered by the fact that in spite of costs rising by 25 per cent over 1939 levels fares were only allowed to rise by less than 17 per cent.

The post war Labour government nationalised the railways from 1 January 1948 and therefore took over the shareholding of East Kent owned by Southern Railway. There had also been plans to nationalise the bus industry but they met with fierce opposition from the BET companies.

Speaking at his last AGM in December 1946, before retirement from the post he had held for 30 years, Chairman Sidney Garcke described the idea as: "Unnecessary and undesirable in the public interest," and said he believed the public was still adequately protected by the Road Traffic Act of 1930.

However, the Tilling owned bus companies sold out in September 1948 to become part of the British Transport Commission. This survived when the Conservatives won power in the general election three years later but remaining plans fell by the wayside.

Although Sidney Garcke stood down as Chairman in 1946, he still retained a place on the East Kent board until his death in October 1948. He was replaced in June 1946 by Raymond Beddow, a leading figure in BET circles since the 1920s. He had been the federation's secretary since 1940 and had joined the boards of several of its subsidiaries including neighbouring Maidstone & District.

55. Book holidays and excursions where you saw this sign. Dozens of agents were appointed by East Kent.

56. East Kent had several enquiry offices of its own – this one is at Margate Harbour. Today, it is the Impressions Café.

57. Double deckers were used at Rye each summer on the Camber to Winchelsea Beach service. EFNs 171 and 173 are pulling away from Rye station in 1964.

There were a number of other senior management changes in the late 1940s, perhaps most notable being Alfred Baynton. He had been company secretary since 1916 and then became general manager from 1942 until taking retirement in 1948.

As the new decade dawned so the costs of rebuilding, higher wages and increased fuel tax pressed East Kent to ask the Traffic Commissioners for permission to raise fares in July 1951. It was the first time the company had applied and, although agreed, it created a lot of hostility among the area's various local newspapers.

Holidaymakers were far from deterred from coming to the area and on Easter Monday in 1950 a check at Charing revealed 65 coaches working between London on either the Dover via Folkestone or Thanet via Canterbury services in only 90 minutes.

During a mid August Saturday in the same year, a record 3,420 passengers were carried between London and Thanet requiring 114 coaches. Around 30 of these had to be

58. One of the wartime utility Guys, now in peacetime livery, outside the Deal enquiry office in the late 1950s. It has just worked a relief from Ramsgate.

59. New in 1950 was a batch of Park Royal bodied Dennis Lancet coaches – used mainly on express or private hire services. This one is seen approaching the new Canterbury bus station after coming through the Riding Gate.

specially hired from independent operators by East Kent.

Hiring additional coaches became a regular practice as the traditional holiday season established itself once more between June and September. Anything up to 60 vehicles would be hired at peak weekends from independents.

As the express business flourished so a new control centre was opened in 1950 at East Kent's office overlooking Ramsgate Harbour to chart the movements of the London to Thanet and South Coast Express services. Sophisticated telephone equipment was installed and the place resembled a wartime RAF operations room.

By now, it was safe to say the coach fleet had returned to a sensible strength and was ready to play a key part in East Kent's revival. Some would say its role was at least as, if not more,

60. Inside the chart room built over the Ramsgate enquiry office in 1950. Sophisticated telephone equipment ensured operators could work efficiently as this contemporary magazine article shows.

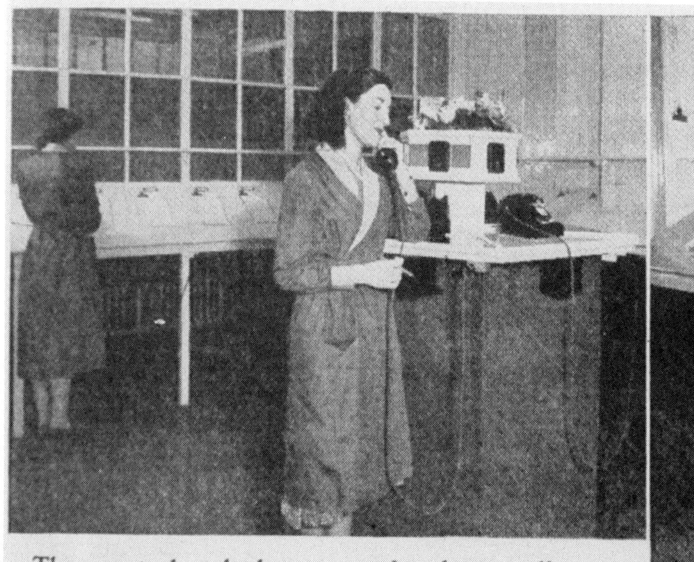

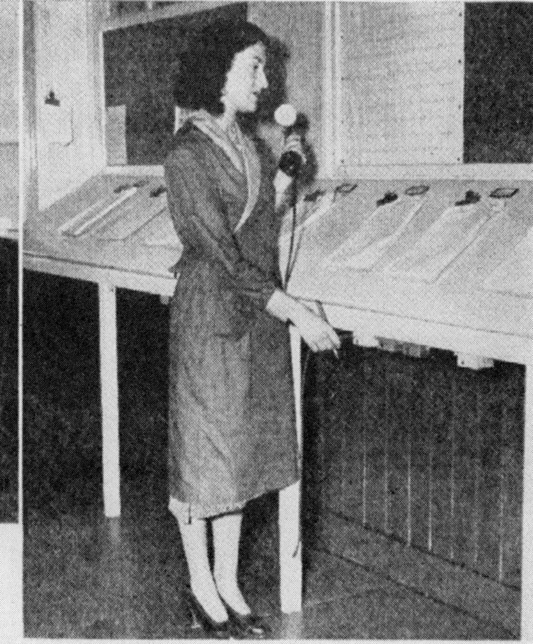

The central telephone stand where calls are received; right, calls are then plugged in by the required chart

61. One of the 1950 32 seat Dennis Lancets was quickly converted to 28 seats as it became the first East Kent vehicle to venture to foreign parts. It stands outside the Hotel Negresco, Nice, in June 1950 with its drivers Gisby and Bushell.

important than operating local stage bus services.

In February 1950 it was decided the company should take on a programme of Continental tours for that summer. It would be the first venture abroad for an East Kent crew and their vehicle. For many passengers it would also be their first time on foreign soil – the British seaside still ruled supreme for holiday choice and cheap flights abroad were unheard of.

During the following three months managers embarked on a frantic programme of inspecting and booking hotels, producing brochures, selecting crews and preparing vehicles, the first one being a brand new half cab Dennis Lancet III with seats for 28 people. Although only built to a standard specification, it proved to be a good choice for the journey offering a smooth, trouble free ride.

The two opening continental tours were 14 days long taking in Paris and the French Riviera. Embarking for the Channel crossing was a tricky exercise as the coach had to be craned aboard the ferry and although the first Townsend roll on, roll off vessel Halladale, wouldn't make its debut at Dover until the following year, coaches were still being lifted in 1953.

The tour drove to the Riviera with stops overnight at Arras, Dijon and Valence before arriving in Nice where five nights were spent at the Hotel Cecil. Visits were made to Monte Carlo and Cannes. The trip homeward consisted of stopovers at Avignon, Vichy, Paris and Amiens.

The exercise was near trouble free save for the loss of two elderly ladies during a 15 minute stop in Lyons. Happily, local gendarmes found them an hour later on the opposite side of the River Rhone.

62. Still giving good service in the early 1950s is this 1935 vintage Leyland Tiger with its 'bandwagon' roofed coach body of 1941. It stands at Folkestone Harbour on an excursion to Deal.

63. Two Swiss misses enjoy the continental café culture on the front cover of the 1959 touring brochure. They are quite oblivious to one of the MJG series AEC Reliances, then the pride of the touring fleet, gliding past.

64. Pictured in 1961 when new at Victoria Coach Station, AEC Reliance WFN 518 wears the light blue Europabus livery in which it was delivered. The vehicle was later used on bus duties and withdrawn in 1977.

The early 1950s saw the first package holidays introduced, notably Global and Blue Cars whose customers would assemble at Victoria coach or railway station. The operators quickly realised that small groups of 30 or so people were more easily managed on coaches and a convenient number for hotels. The usual arrangement was for a coach to carry the groups from London to embark at Dover Marine and be met by a Continental coach at Calais or Boulogne for the tour itself.

By 1953 a new contract with Europabus had been agreed. Europabus was a company formed by Continental railways to provide coach links between rail and road termini. The new contract offered a coach journey from Victoria to Dover with East Kent, a ferry crossing to Ostend enabling passengers to board Europabus vehicles for Frankfurt.

Take up was slow in the beginning with only 182 bookings that summer but there was more success the following year when London Coastal Coaches, who owned Victoria Coach station, became agents in the capital.

East Kent took an instrumental role in another new continental service in 1954 when it took on the job of carrying passengers for the London to Lympne Airport, near Hythe, leg of Coach-Air's flights to Paris. Flying to Beauvais on a 32 seat Skyways Dakota, passengers were then taken on French coaches to Paris 60 miles and a two hour ride away. The overall journey time from London to Paris was six hours and the fare £7 14 shillings (£7.70) return at off peak periods, which was actually slightly less than the British Railways third class fare combining trains and channel ferry.

Skyways planned to run 21 departures a day in each direction in the high season but it is not thought this ambitious figure was achieved. In the years that followed Skyways opened up additional services to six more destinations including Amsterdam.

65. The Skyways Coach-Air service began in April 1954 and was operated with Leyland Royal Tigers.

66. Just heading out of East Kent's depot in the centre of Ashford is a 58 seater Guy Arab IV. Registered in 1953, it is serving a town route extended to the Batchelor's factory at shift times.

Although the 1950s is regarded by many as a golden time for East Kent, gradual social changes during the decade combined with more fare increases would store up problems for the future.

Widespread TV ownership meant that people who previously thought nothing of visiting the cinema a couple of times a week stayed at home instead. Many of them had travelled to and from their local Gaumont, Odeon or ABC on the bus of course. ITV's arrival mid way through the decade only exacerbated the situation – it's interesting to note that BET had a major holding in Rediffusion, one of the early ITV companies.

Meanwhile, new cars – no longer being built exclusively for export – were now flooding on to the home market and within the reach of many for the first time willing to buy them on hire purchase schemes. These changes inevitably had a knock on effect over a period of time and saw early and late evening services in particular being cut back.

Once the initial post war problems had been solved an order for 80 Guy Arabs was delivered in 1950 and 1951 with 30 more in 1952 and 1953 and another 25 in 1956 and 1957. The first batch were lowbridge specified and came with Gardner 6LW engines. The 1951 and 1953 batches carried Park Royal's highbridge bodies with 56 seats and a curved front profile resembling the London RT. The 1953 batch were fitted with folding doors on the rear platform as were th last batch with a different body design seating 61 passengers.

67. 'Feathers in our caps' were the enigmatic words cast into the head dress of the Red Indian chief which adorned the radiators of Guy buses for many years.

68. Another of the 1953 delivery of Guy buses with Park Royal bodies poses in front of the Klinger sock and stocking factory at Margate. The vehicle worked until 1971 while a DIY store now stands on the site of the factory.

69. A 1957 registered Guy Arab IV, again with Park Royal body work, operates the Betteshanger Colliery workmen's service in Dover. The journey from Dover to the mine involved several stops and took 35 minutes.

70. From the second batch of Weymann bodied AEC Reliances was this 41 seater. Delivered in 1956, it was initially used as a coach before being directed to bus duties, as seen here on the Hythe town service at Saltwood.

The latest innovation in bus design was the underfloor engine and most of the major chassis builders had worked out new designs by the mid 1950s. Repositioning the engine away from the front gave space for another six passengers. The entrance door could be placed at the front ahead of the wheels to allow one man operation – or OMO as it quickly became known – but this wouldn't catch on in a big way for a few more years yet.

The floods of early 1953, which devastated much of eastern England, tested the company's

71. One of the most rural of East Kent's terminal points was Westmarsh on the 74 service from Sandwich. A one man operated CFN 114 – converted in 1959 – awaits the occasional passenger during 1961.

72. Body builder Park Royal was glad to have East Kent's business and featured one of the new Reliances in a trade advertisement. Ramsgate Harbour appears in the background.

mettle. A plea for urgent help came from British Railways on Sunday 1 February resulting in all available staff preparing 30 coaches which had been in winter storage at St Peter's. They were required to run a shuttle service between Birchington and Faversham, long stretches of the line having been completely washed away. By the end of that month a total of 44 vehicles had been used to replace trains and had clocked up around 720,000 miles. For some time after, another 20 buses were also hired to carry workmen rebuilding the breached sea defences.

Bad weather again caused havoc during the tough winter of 1956 when for 19 days life was made unpleasant by blizzards, snow and ice. Some 48 routes were closed or diverted and vehicles were either ditched or trapped on 140 occasions. On nine of these nights buses were simply abandoned where they stopped.

East Kent's allegiance to Dennis vehicles ended when it decided to purchase 40 Weymann bodied AEC Reliance single deckers in 1955. These were built for dual purpose use as bus or coach depending on seasonal demand and could carry 41 passengers, 10 of these had OMO capability. Another 22 arrived the following year. In 1957 a third batch of 39 dual purpose models arrived and in actual fact, saw more coach use than the earlier ones.

These vehicles would form the backbone of the South Coast Express service and be a familiar sight on country bus routes for anything up to 20 years, well into the nationalisation era.

73. A selection of East Kent timetables from the 1950s.

74. The new Bouverie Square bus station takes shape in early 1955.

The mid 1950s saw two of the company's principal bus stations entirely rebuilt. First was Folkestone's Bouverie Square. Work had begun in the summer of 1954 with completion in 1955.

In the same year construction commenced at St George's Lane, Canterbury, on a replacement for the by now cramped station at the West Gate end of St Peter's Place. At this time much of the centre of the city was either being, or had been earmarked for, redevelopment as part of post war regeneration. In all some 33 acres of the centre had been identified as required for compulsory purchase to carry out the local authority's ambitious new schemes – including the St Peter's Place site for a ring road.

75. Inside the travel office at Bouverie Square shortly after opening.

76. An aerial view of the completed Folkestone bus station in 1956.

77. Guests gather to place a commemorative plaque as work begins on Canterbury bus station in May 1955. 78. East Kent's Chairman Raymond Beddow and city Mayor Alderman HP Dawton admire the stone.

The company was very annoyed, not surprisingly, at the prospect of losing its bus station, especially as no alternative had been offered. However, management did have its eye on a strip of blitzed land between St George's Lane and St George's Terrace but the council had ruled out putting a bus station within the city walls.

Both sides were ready for a battle but the council blinked first, realising its ring road plans would be held up for a long time if East Kent

79. An architect's model of how the Canterbury bus station would look – made long before the arrival of computer aided design. The offices were meant to resemble the side of an East Kent coach.

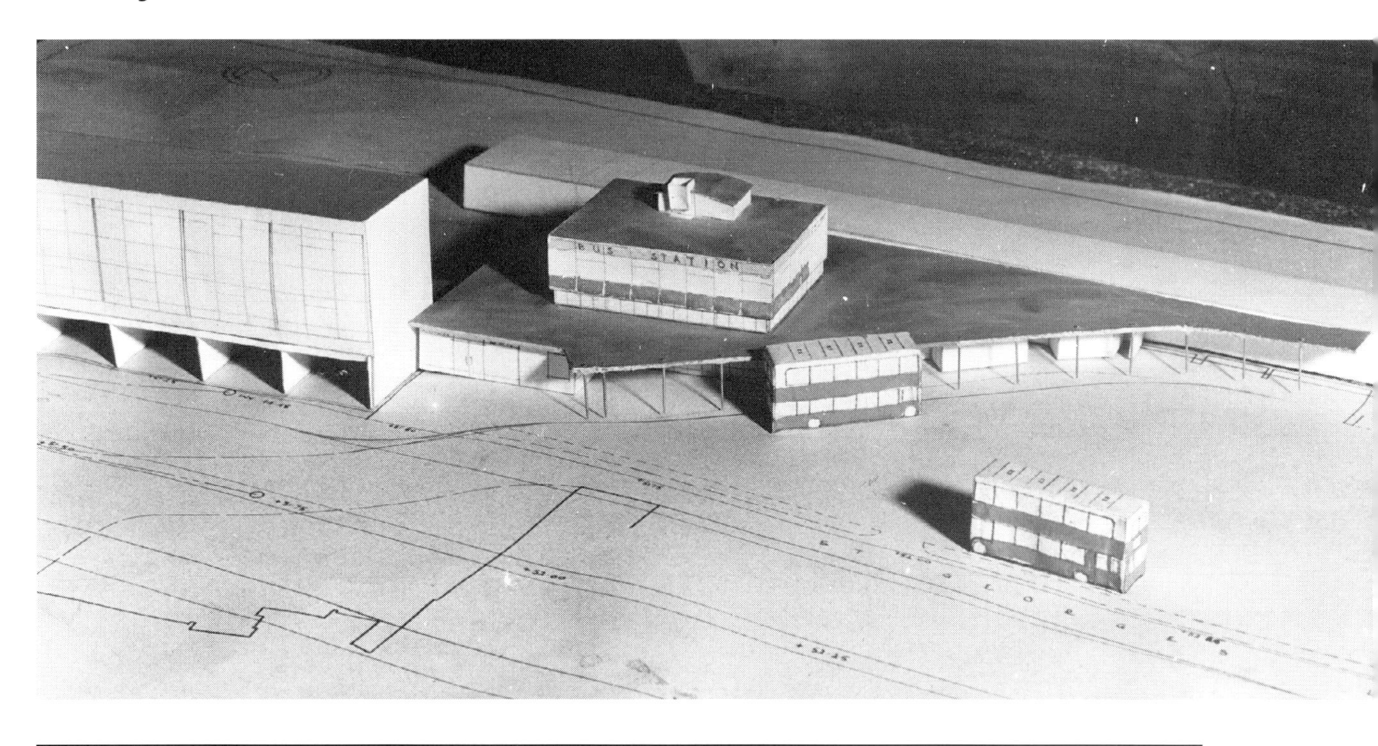

80. Workmen lay the concrete sections which would eventually form the bus station's large apron. In the far corner the steel work of the office structure has been erected.

were to fight the St Peter's Place purchase. The only land it could offer in return was a site to the east of St George's Lane. This had been acquired on compulsory purchase earlier in the decade and besides, Whitehall had decreed East Kent should have its new bus station inside the walls.

So it came to pass that Chairman Raymond Beddow and the Mayor, Alderman HP Dawton, were able to bring a happy ending to the saga, laying a large stone plaque on 10 May 1955 to officially mark the start of construction.

The £70,000 scheme took a year to complete and saw a wide concrete apron form the centre of the station with shelters running along the sides. Offices, built to resemble the side of an East Kent coach, were located at one end, nearest the city centre.

The first live departure from the new bus station was a Thanet based AEC Reliance coach, KFN 211, driven by EN Sturips on Sunday 6 May 1956 travelling to London.

81. Opening day at Canterbury bus station on Sunday 6 May 1956 and already plenty of buses are awaiting passengers.

82. A good natured group of striking East Kent staff man a picket line at Canterbury in 1957.

Extensive work was also carried out at Russell Street, Dover, on two occasions during the 1950s including raising the roof height to enable high-bridge vehicles to lodge there. New underground fuel storage tanks were installed in late 1958. Capable of holding 30,000 gallons of diesel the company noted, with dismay, that represented £3,750 worth of duty for the Chancellor!

On a less happy note, East Kent and its staff found themselves caught up in a national bus strike in 1957. The normally friendly relations between company and workforce took a blow as drivers and conductors felt obliged to withdraw their labour for nine days in July. An extra £1 per week was being sought in the national claim but operators were only offering an additional three shillings (15p). Unions felt insulted but a compromise was eventually reached.

83. Investment was made in the company's infrastructure as this pristine shelter at Wingham demonstrates.

84. In the late 1950s work was carried out at Russell Street, Dover, to sink new underground fuel tanks.

85. The PFN Regents spent most of their lives at Thanet and would always be associated with the 49, 50 and 52 services which enjoyed a six minute headway in the high summer.

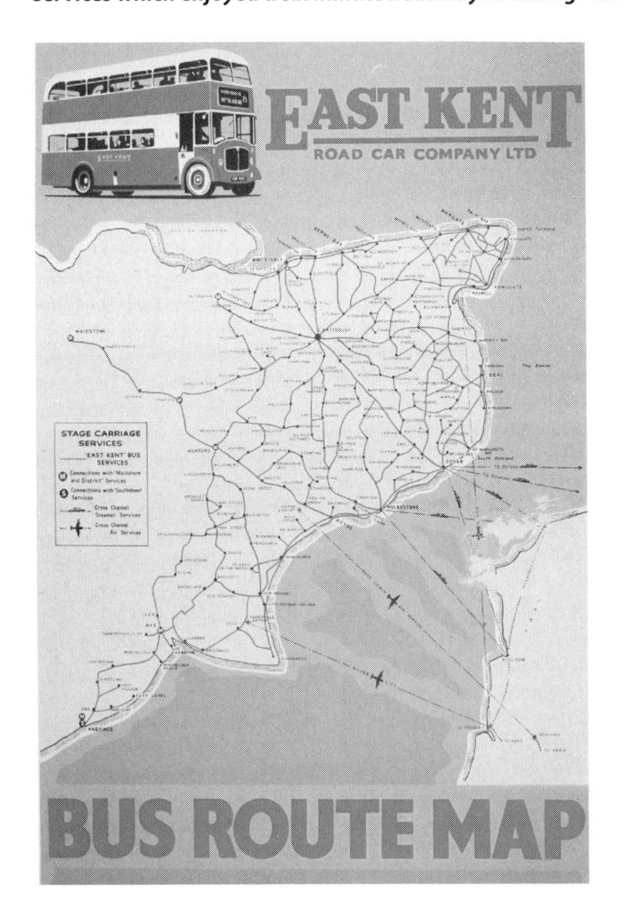

86. The Puffin bus adorns this 1960 bus route map. A success for East Kent, few were used elsewhere.

As the last 40 utility style Guys came up for replacement, an order was placed for 40 AEC Regent Mk Vs, thus completing the switch to that marque following the earlier single decker orders. The Park Royal bodied vehicles, built to the newly permitted 30 feet length and capable of carrying 72 passengers, duly arrived in summer 1959 and were immediately distinguished by their front entrances and full fronted cabs.

They entered service in Thanet, where many would be based for most of their working lives, but during winter periods were also used on inter-urban routes around Canterbury and Herne Bay.

They were all given registrations beginning PFN and consequently earned the nickname of Puffins. While these vehicles were a success for East Kent, comparatively few were used elsewhere.

The summer season of 1959 saw the introduction of the first open top buses along the east Kent coast. Considering the company relied so heavily on seasonal trade, it's a little surprising this hadn't happened long before. Other operators on the south coast such as Eastbourne Corporation, Southdown, Brighton Hove & District had identified a market for the seasonal open topper several years earlier.

Cutting the roofs off six vintage utility Guys and repainting them all over cream with a red waist band – the reverse of the traditional East Kent paint job – they were introduced on services 56 and 69 in Thanet and proved to be an immediate success. Three years later an open top service 44 was introduced in Herne Bay. As these already elderly vehicles finally wore out, they were replaced by more specially converted Guys and the Thanet services became one, route 69, in 1969 following the opening of the Hoverport at Pegwell Bay. Riding the entire 16 mile route on the top deck from Minnis Bay to Pegwell Bay and back was an annual summer treat for many – including the author! Dover, Folkestone and Hythe also had their own open toppers from 1968 to 1971, running as far as St Mary's Bay at one stage.

86. Newly converted Guy utility open topper wends its way past Ramsgate Harbour.

87. By the time this Guy Arab was photographed near Ramsgate Harbour in May 1972, it had already seen three seasons on the coastal service.

88. *East Kent's new HQ building in Station Road West.*

The company moved to a new headquarters building in Station Road West, Canterbury, in 1960 enabling Odsal House at Harbledown – a 'temporary' home for the previous 14 years – to be vacated.

East Kent ordered dozens more AEC Regents between 1961 and 1967, gradually building up to a total of 121. They differed from the earlier ones by having half cabs and jack knife folding doors. There were also three low height Bridgemaster models, about a foot lower than the others, which were used on Dover's route 129 which included a low railway bridge. Regent batches delivered in 1961 and 1962 were fitted with illuminated panels on the driver's side of the vehicle to add more impact at night for advertisements.

Two more batches, 40 and 19, of the AEC Reliance single deckers were also purchased as dual purpose vehicles and arrived in 1960 and 1961, all with 41 seat bodywork by East Kent's favourite Park Royal.

Investment in new coaches continued during the 1960s for continental holiday, express, excursion and private hire work. The first 36 feet

89. Ten of the 1966 Regents were delivered new to Ashford. GJG 744D pulls away on a town service via the High Street.

90. AEC Regent V WFN 841 was little more than a year old when it crashed off the Herne Bay road in 1962. Despite this, it stayed in service until the mid 1970s.

91. One of the GFN series Guys took a tumble along the Elham Valley road in April 1961. Help is at hand from East Kent's own recovery truck.

long vehicles made their debut in 1962 in the form of 20 AEC Reliances with 46 seater Park Royal bodies, driven by 9.5 litre engines. A dozen of these were painted in the sky blue livery of Europabus. Another four batches of similar vehicles were delivered between 1963 and 1966, adding another 58 to the fleet, the later ones distinguished by fewer but larger windows and forced air ventilation.

92. Steady as she goes. One of the 36 feet long AEC Reliance coaches undergoes the tilt test in 1962.

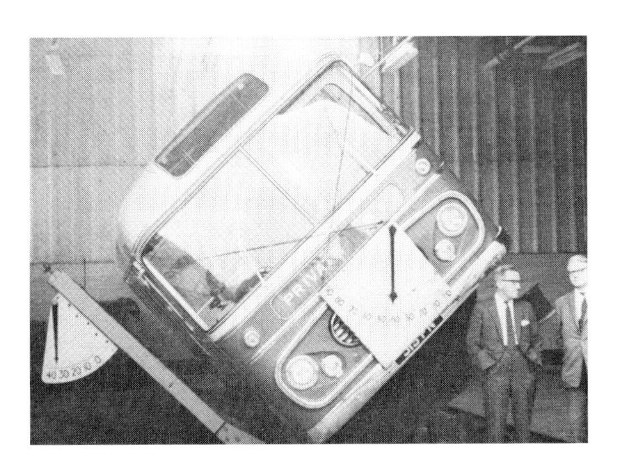

The 1962 models were the first of their type to be bodied by Park Royal and therefore one of them had to be tilt tested for stability. This involved tipping the vehicle to 35 degrees or more as required by the Ministry of Transport to be considered safe. Just to make sure it was as authentic as possible, each seat was packed with weights of 140lbs to represent the typical bulk of a passenger.

93. The same Reliance faces the wrong way around for a photo outside Canterbury bus station.

94 and 95. Guy Arab MFN 901 was delivered in 1956 and entered service the following year. From 1959 to 1962 it was used each winter as a publicity vehicle touring the Midlands promoting the South East for sunny holidays.

96. A virtually deserted M2 motorway would have ensured a trouble free run for this coach as it headed for London in 1963 soon after the road's completion.

97. The journey to London for this Reliance would have been far from trouble free in the same year. Snow and a piece of wood in the radiator grille at Canterbury's Wincheap are clearly the causes of the problem!

98. A very busy day at London's Victoria Coach Station one morning in summer 1964 as passengers for the Continent frantically prepare to board at least 20 East Kent coaches – of varying types – bound for Dover.

99. One of the Duple Commander bodied continental touring coaches. The current owner of this vehicle plans to have it back on the road in 2006.

The Duple Commander body, also mounted on AEC Reliance chassis, made its first appearance in East Kent in 1964, a combination widely used by BET Group companies at this time.

Industrial relations between company, trades unions and staff remained reasonably good barring an unofficial strike and working to rule in early 1965 over a national pay and conditions claim.

In common with airlines, railways and other bus operators, East Kent adopted the 24 hour clock in its timetables during 1965.

Its staff magazine East Kent Omnibus stated, optimistically perhaps: "Timetables will be far easier to read and passengers will be able to check on the bus they want twice as quickly, twice as surely. In future it will be impossible to to misread a timetable by mistaking an am arrival for a pm one or vice versa. No longer will there be any doubt about it."

100. Ticket machine poised, an East Kent conductress shows off her style for 1966.

East Kent's golden jubilee was marked in 1966 and gave the management a chance to reflect on the previous 50 years achievements and challenges.

A souvenir brochure stated: "Operating buses has become vastly more complicated and each year has brought its own particular problems – human, technical and financial problems affecting the lives of hundreds of thousands of Kentish people. The company can fairly claim that its jubilee is proof that it has solved satisfactorily many of the problems it has had to face over the years."

Quite properly observing that the company's jubilee could not have been reached without the help of the staff, the brochure noted that 442 past and present employees had completed more than 25 years service. Of these, 117 had clocked up at least 40 years, the majority still actually working.

101. Taken for the golden jubilee souvenir brochure of 1966, this aerial view of Canterbury bus station is all the more remarkable for the lack of traffic on the city ring road.

In fact, the first 50 year service award was made at the company's jubilee celebration lunch. Reg Taylor, a lathe operator at the Canterbury Central Works, received, at his own choosing, a new gas cooker from Ray Beddow just a week or two before his well deserved retirement.

Reg said at the time: "Goodness knows I shall miss East Kent badly – it has been my whole life and I'll probably take a part time job to keep active."

The lunch itself was held at the Grand Hotel, Folkestone, on 4 October 1966 and the 200 guests invited by the directors included mayors and civic leaders from all of the towns in East Kent, traffic commissioners, police, major suppliers and journalists. There was also a special place for former general manager Alfred Baynton who had retired in 1948.

102. Reg Taylor, a lathe operator at the Central Works, was the first East Kent employee to achieve 50 years service. He chose a new gas cooker as his gift.

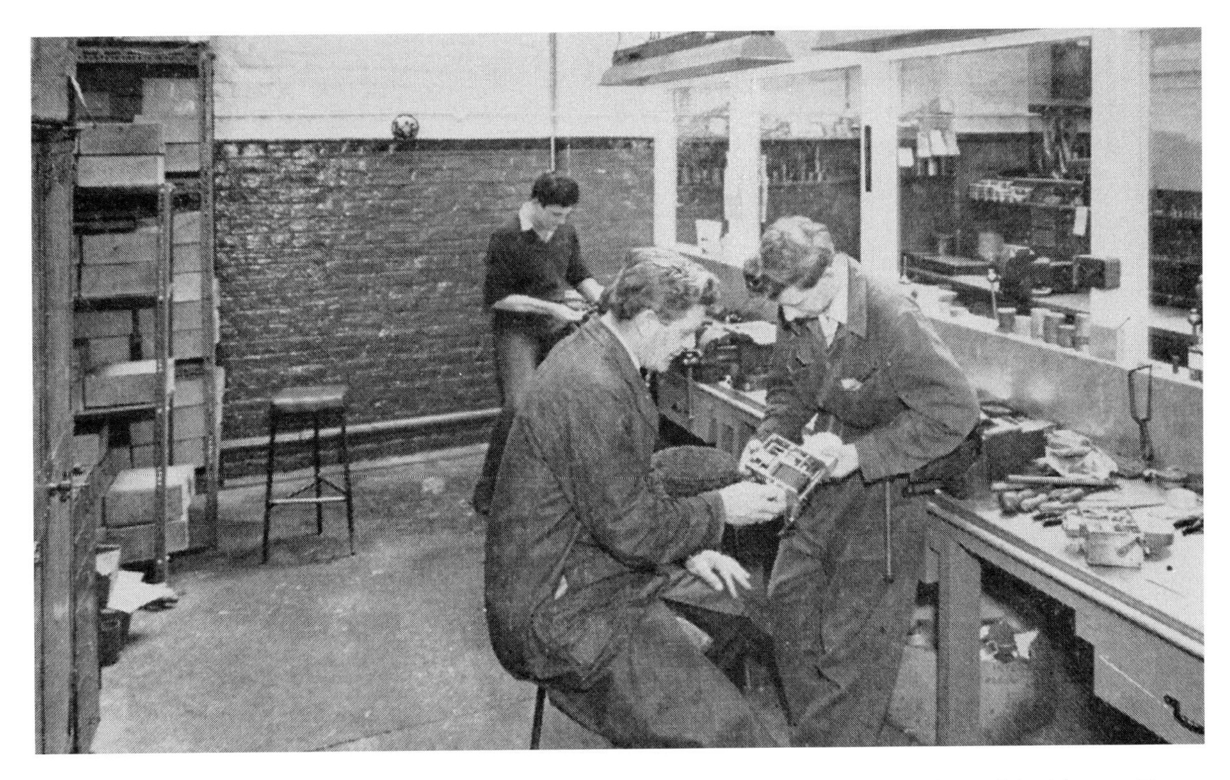

103. A new home was created in 1966 at Canterbury Central Works for mechanics maintaining the Setright ticket machines.

By 1966 the company employed 2,160 people with a fleet of 622 vehicles used to carry 60 million passengers. Its 137 services amounted to more than 1,000 route miles.

Social changes were continuing to bite though and the company found its profits sliding in the mid sixties. Wage increases in May 1965 contributed to a fall of nearly £30,000 in profits in 1965 along with tax and national insurance rises. New legislation governing how income tax

104. In the fibre glass shop at Canterbury. Note the variety of items which could be produced here.

105. Installing a crypton test bench in 1966 enabled testing of electrical units under operating style conditions.

was paid on share dividends from 1966 swallowed up another £60,000 while the following year a late delivery of new vehicles led to reduced capital allowances – the amount which can be claimed back from the Inland Revenue for investing in new plant.

The national picture for the bus industry looked increasingly gloomy as the decade neared its end. It had become caught in a spiral of falling passenger numbers and increased costs prompting fare increases, which in turn drove people away from bus travel. East Kent was no exception and it too faced falls in revenue and service cut backs.

The Labour government of the day espoused common ownership of a variety of national industries and was keen to extend that to the parts of the bus industry which were not already part of its British Transport Commission.

Despite some tough talking by the top brass of East Kent's parent BET, they finally threw in the towel in November 1967 and agreed to sell to the commission all the bus and coach interests in England and Wales for £47 million.

The sale was greeted with shock by individual BET company general managers. The first they knew of the decision was when they received phone calls telling them an item would be appearing on that night's television news announcing the sale.

106. Winner of the Miss East Kent 1967 title was Margaret Knight, representing the Dover depot. She won Premium Bonds and had the honour of leading the company's annual grand parade held at Margate's Winter Gardens.

107. East Kent staff were able to enjoy a network of thriving depot based social clubs. One of the highlights of the year was the Miss East Kent contest with young women from each club competing for the overall title. Here are the finalists of the 1968 competition gathered on the steps of the headquarters building after judging by a panel of 'experts'.

108. The conductors' paying in room at Westwood depot.

109. A busy summer's day at Dymchurch bus station in August 1971. Even the relief AEC Regent – from the last batch delivered to East Kent – is filling fast. Meanwhile, a Guy open topper is also doing brisk trade.

110. A 1968 Marshall bodied AEC Reliance has just turned through Birchington Square in the August of that year on its way from Ramsgate to Minnis Bay towards the end of the rural route 70 in Thanet.

111. This Westwood based Daimler Fleetline, one of the company's first rear engined double deckers, is in Cecil Square, Margate, on the Garlinge to Dane Valley service.

The nationalised era

AFTER a period of time in which East Kent and the other newly nationalised former BET components were held by the specially created Transport Holding Company, the National Bus Company took over control as it came into being on 1 January 1969.

These would be times of great change with senior personnel being moved from one company to another bringing greater integration between operators.

Raymond Beddow, only the second Chairman of East Kent since 1916, took the opportunity to retire in early 1968 as his health deteriorated.

Writing in the staff magazine Omnibus he said: "Some years have been good and some not so good. All in all it (East Kent) has given good and faithful service to the public and I am confident it will continue to do so."

Out on the roads, efforts to convert services to one man operation had been gathering pace during the run up to nationalisation. They took

112. An Alexander bodied AEC Swift, one of the last to be delivered in traditional East Kent livery, makes its way along South Road, Tower Hamlets in Dover.

113. A small selection of the many sign boards used by East Kent's enquiry offices and agents in the area advertising excursions and express services.

on a new urgency afterwards when the Ministry of Transport started giving grants, of up to 50 per cent in some cases, to enable operators to buy buses particularly suited for the task.

Accordingly, for 1969 East Kent ordered 20 Daimler Fleetline double deckers and 10 AEC Swift single deckers, marking in both types the first rear engined vehicles of the fleet. Ten of the 72 seater Daimlers arrived ready for OMO working while the remainder were converted shortly after delivery. All served in Thanet, becoming a familiar sight on the island's roads for years after, and would wear traditional cherry and cream livery until the mid 1970s.

The very last buses to be delivered new in traditional East Kent colours were another batch of 12 AEC Swifts arriving in 1971 with Alexander W type OMO bodywork.
Most were based at Dover for their 16 year long careers.

114. Colourful excursion leaflets were printed for almost every occasion. These are a few dating from 1971.

115. With the exception of three one man operated PFNs at Rye, all other depots confined their OMO Regents to peak hour and relief workings. Dover's GJG 759D will shortly pick up schoolchildren going home to Eastry and Sandwich.

One man operation represented a major opportunity to cut labour costs, making the familiar conductor an endangered species. Services in a number of areas had been closely reviewed in the late 1960s and weekend and evening operating had been cut back by now to stem heavy losses.

In its rush to OMO working, East Kent acquired 30 Leyland Leopard single deckers from Southdown in 1971. New in 1963 and 1964, they survived for another six years, mainly in Folkestone, and were extensively refurbished along the way. By 1971 Dover and Folkestone garages were equipped solely with OMO buses, many of them converted AEC Regents, while Deal followed suit in 1972.

Management took a long hard look at its by now ageing collection of single deckers, including more than 100 AEC Reliances dating from the 1950s and working beyond their intended life span. At the same time, the last rear platform entry double deckers were phased out along with some of the early AEC Regents.

Major orders for the newly introduced Leyland National single decker were placed. Designed as a joint venture between NBC and British Leyland with the modern operator in mind, they were distinguished by their curved front windscreens and wedge shaped air conditioning units mounted on the rear of the roof. They were also

116. Thirty Marshall bodied Leyland Leopards were acquired from Southdown in 1971 to help with the introduction of one man operation in the Folkestone area. 278 AUF passes through Lydd.

117. Seen here as a preserved vehicle, this was one of the 100 or more AEC Reliances which came under the microscope in the early 1970s. It actually stayed in service until 1976.

noted for their impressive turn of speed – the growing amount of traffic would not be held up too long by slow moving buses any longer! With a capacity of 60-plus passengers, this was only a handful fewer than the double deckers, making the Nationals an attractive proposition for routes where passenger numbers were dwindling.

The trend for single deckers was underlined by the fact there would be no more double deckers added to the fleet until 1976, a gap of seven years – the previous buses being Thanet's Daimler Fleetlines.

118. Still a familiar sight on the streets of east Kent in the 1970s were bus stop flags like these.

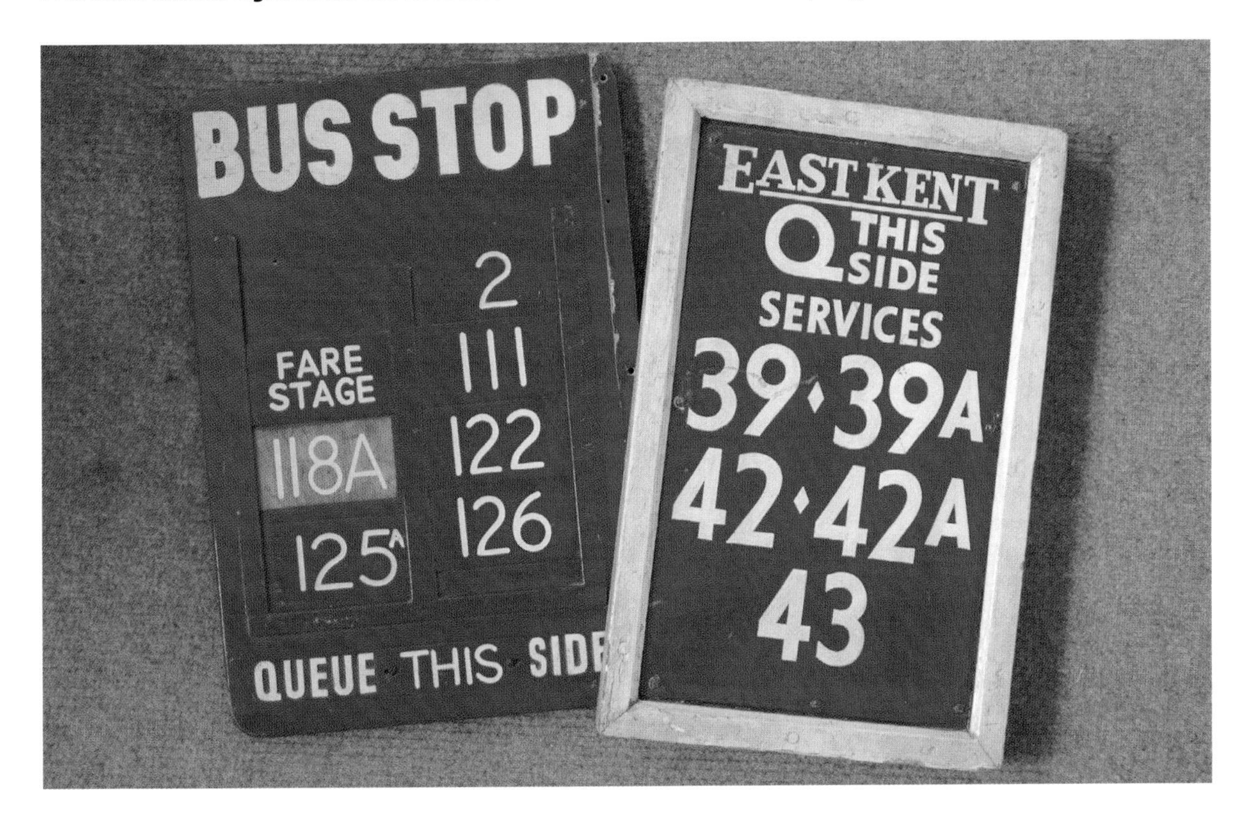

119. Leyland National EFN 168L was delivered to East Kent in 1973 and is seen here bound for Folkestone. All new buses being delivered wore the NBC poppy red livery. The service had by now been renumbered 590.

All of East Kent's latest purchases bore the NBC poppy red livery, a colour which jarred in the purists' eye, more used to cherry and cream. From 1972, a repainting programme began to apply the poppy red to the existing fleet but it was noted the new colour had an unfortunate tendency to fade to a strange shade of orange after a year or two's hard wear and tear.

East Kent had started to work more closely with Maidstone & District right from the beginning of nationalisation and one of the ways this manifested itself was with the closure of the Hastings depot in September 1969 and the transfer of its two services to M&D. East Kent was pulling out of the town after 35 years, its purpose built garage at Coghurst having only been built in 1961. Schedules had remained unchanged in many years for the six buses and 12 staff based here. Drivers knew their passengers well and their exact setting down points. A small dormitory base at Lydd also ceased and its work was taken over by New Romney.

Realignments continued in March 1973 when operations at Rye, including the depot itself, were transferred to M&D control. In May, M&D closed down its operations in Ashford. In practice the two companies had all but merged there two years previously and East Kent simply took over the remaining routes. In December M&D took over East Kent's interests in Faversham as well.

All of these changes prompted a review of the route numbering system, largely unaltered since 1937 and by now proving restrictive. Routes in Ashford were given new numbers in the 500s, while it was intended that 100s would be allocated to Canterbury routes, 200s for Thanet

120. East Kent's Coghurst garage in Hastings, seen after completion in 1961, was sold by the company eight years later when services in Hastings were handed over to Maidstone & District shortly after nationalisation.

121. An AEC Regent, resplendent in NBC poppy red, at Canterbury bus station, blinded for the University service.

services, 300s for Deal and Dover and 400s for Folkestone. However, this plan wasn't fully introduced as it was realised there would be clashes with M&D services.

Passenger numbers continued downwards but new legislation requiring county councils, including Kent and East Sussex, to consult with bus operators to develop coordinated and efficient public transport systems – and, crucially, continue to subsidise them – brought considerable relief in 1972.

Just how much public transport operators benefited is illustrated by the fact that in March 1976, the level of grants stood at £286,000 – the lion's share going to East Kent and M&D – but by 1984 this had climbed nearly ten fold to £2,773,000.

The early 1970s saw difficult economic conditions for all, centring around rocketing inflation, rising unemployment as well as the three day week and miners' strike of 1973. Once again these events would lead to higher fares for passengers and services being curtailed.

Integration with M&D saw that company's senior personnel transfer to Canterbury to new combined headquarters in North Lane in 1979. While building work was being carried out here, an old Roman burial ground was found. The Station Road West office was subsequently vacated and sold. During the late 1990s it was converted into town apartments.

On the coaching front, discussions had started on the feasibility of creating a nationwide network immediately upon nationalisation. It wasn't until 1973 that National Travel (NBC) Ltd came into being, regionalised into five areas. From October, East Kent's coaches formed part of the 140 vehicle strong National Travel (South East) fleet responsible for providing express services.

The move saw all the coaches repainted into corporate white, much to the indignation of the individual companies concerned. Reticent about the move anyway – they had after all been successfully operating coach services for many years without outside interference – another new colour scheme was the last straw.

122. East Kent acquired a number of Metro-Cammell bodied Leyland Atlanteans from Maidstone & District in 1973 when it took over operations in Ashford. This one is seen in Maidstone town centre.

Office based technology finally caught up with East Kent in the 1970s when computerisation dawned. It meant that a particular quirk of the company came to an end – a fleet numbering system was introduced in 1977.

Ever since formation the company had managed without fleet numbering, and in post war years aimed to ensure the digits in registration numbers of new vehicles were seldom duplicated. Thus whole series of registrations would be block booked with the authorities when delivery dates became known.

Necessity for change arose when merging the maintenance records of all vehicles on to the same system as those of M&D vehicles. In fact spare sequences of M&D numbers were used so that the two series of single and double deckers and coaches would match.

In late 1978 National Bus Company chiefs kick-started a series of studies of how buses were being used up and down the country to enable networks to meet local needs. East Kent and M&D were included in the scheme.

The two year long task involved recruiting dozens of part time workers and they interviewed passengers at bus stations and others while making house to house calls, to complete forms over their usage – or non-usage – of local transport, covering issues such as fares, frequency and length of journey. Virtually every route was closely scrutinised as a result.

The exercise, named Market Analysis Project, proved timely as more social shifts began to take their effect in the late 1970s and early 1980s. There continued to be significant increases in car

123. Resting up at Dover between school duties are an AEC Regent and, behind it, one of the Alexander bodied AEC Swifts.

124. One of the Thanet based Daimler Fleetlines nears its Ramsgate Harbour destination.

ownership – more people buying a second vehicle – and out of town shopping centres were becoming more popular. This concentrated bus use over shorter periods of time, yet dispersing it across a wider area.

Management now worked hard to match the route network to meet as many of the needs identified by the survey's data as it could. Each proposal was discussed with Kent County Council – now, thanks to its subsidies – the biggest 'customer' of East Kent's services.

Passengers saw many positive benefits including several through links on services while cutbacks included closing the depot in Albert

125. Pensioners were able to enjoy out of season coach holidays with East Kent for much of the 1970s.

126. A Plaxton Elite bodied AEC Reliance coach, wearing the white NBC livery, rounds the Eiffel Tower in 1976.

127. By 1976 East Kent staff had been kitted out with NBC corporate uniforms as modelled here by June Redford, one of seven women drivers at Westwood depot in Thanet. Daimler Fleetline RFN 960G provides a suitable backdrop.

128. No-passport excursions to France and Belgium were popular tours for East Kent in the 1970s.

Road, Deal. For some this was a sad move as this is where the first bus services in east Kent had begun 70 years earlier.

As Margaret Thatcher's Conservative government swept to power in May 1979 so the first hints of more radical changes in the bus industry emerged. In the election campaign the party had pledged to curb the powers of the Traffic Commissioners, the regulators who had licensed vehicles, crews, routes and approved fare increases for nearly half a century.

By November the government had published a White Paper outlining a new Transport Bill. Despite opposition – some of it from the Tory benches – the Bill became law by October 1980.

The effects of this new piece of legislation saw public service vehicle licensing replaced by operator licensing. Certificates of Fitness for vehicles, issued for up to seven years depending on the condition of the bus, were superseded by regulations insisting vehicles undergo an annual test at an authorised station.

Definitions of express and stage services changed as well. From October 1981 a road service licence was required only for ordinary bus (stage) services. These became any local operation for which fares were charged and the route being less than 50 kms. Express services were deemed to be those travelling at least 50 kms and could be scheduled services, excursions or tours.

The 1980 and 1981 period was a traumatic time for East Kent as it continued to struggle to keep down costs. Upheavals at this time saw bus services extensively revised, depots, workshops and offices closed. Many staff were made redundant as the one man operation programme reached completion in August 1981.

As a result of the cost cutting, the company saved nearly £1.5 million against its 1980 budget of £30.5 million while revenue stayed about the same.

Plans by Kent County Council to cut its subsidies on loss making but vital routes threatened to make things worse in 1982 but a

129. East Kent took an active role in the National Holidays network with neighbouring subsidiaries.

booklet, issued by East Kent and M&D, entitled The Route to a Healthy Future proved an invaluable public relations tool.

Explaining to county councillors as well as the travelling public how the merger of the two operators had helped reduce costs and increase efficiency during the previous 10 years, it also stressed great care had been taken to preserve the autonomy of the two organisations and retain their own fleet names and liveries.

Happily, after lengthy negotiations and extensive reading of the route booklet, KCC relented on its plans and decided to reduce only half of the subsidies it had originally intended.

Express coach services offered some relief amid the gloom and by the end of 1979 there were more than 20 scheduled departures from the East Kent area to London every day, setting out from Ramsgate, Margate, Deal, Dover and Herne Bay. Particularly popular as a starting point was Dover Eastern Docks where 14 departures for London were made daily. Cross Channel sailings prompted a small coach station to be created at the docks where an inspector would meet Continental arrivals to deal with bus or coach enquiries and issue tickets for the National Express network.

The 1980 Transport Act enabled coach operators to offer commuter services for people working in London. Two such routes were introduced in November 1980 departing from Folkestone and Herne Bay. The latter would leave Beltinge at 6.05am and take nearly two and a half hours to reach Victoria Coach Station.

130. Bristol VRTs bearing Eastern Coachworks bodies joined the East Kent fleet in 1976. This one operates the long distance service between Folkestone and Maidstone.

131. In 1983/4 East Kent had ten Reliance chassis rebodied by Dutch builders Berkhof including this one seen at Canterbury. All of the contingent had been withdrawn by 1990.

Time wise, it wasn't competitive with the trains but for the annual price of £629, offered a considerable saving. The Herne Bay route did prove a success and survived for 10 years.

In May 1983 NBC split East Kent from M&D in a bid to inject vitality into the two companies. East Kent's central works in Canterbury was hived off to form a separate entity – Kent Engineering Ltd – with M&D's unit at Hawkhurst. Forty head office jobs were lost and the management structure altered to divide the traffic function into separate commercial and operating groups.

The philosophy now was that the company would do everything in house more cheaply than using outside contractors, buying in only specialist services when absolutely necessary. All work had to be costed carefully before being allowed to go ahead. Some mistakes were made when it was discovered that replacing the element of an office kettle cost more than double the price of buying a whole new kettle. There would be no more French polishing of desks either when a bill for £456 arrived after one at the former central works was revitalised in this way!

Just as East Kent became a separate entity once more, so NBC's subsidy scheme for capital investments ended and therefore no new buses arrived that year. However, much needed investment on coaches was made with five 53 seater Leyland Tigers with Plaxton bodies being ordered. Five MCW Metroliners, the first of their kind, came to East Kent to help update the National Holidays fleet at the same time.

Ten AEC Reliance coaches were given new bodies, effectively bringing new vehicles for half the price, during 1983/4. While rebodying was nothing new, this latest scheme did bring unforeseen problems. The new bodies were half a ton heavier than previous and meant vehicle performance was sluggish and led to engines overheating. An air based power steering system installed in these particular coaches also proved less than perfect.

The miners' strike of 1984 added to the company's financial problems. The National Coal Board had long been a contract customer for whom East Kent provided workmen's services to the area's four collieries at one time or another. During the year long strike East Kent missed out on £250,000 of revenue and was unable to redeploy buses and drivers to other duties in the belief that an end was always near.

In a bid to keep down overheads, the company announced a proposal to close the Canterbury depot and introduce a number of outstations in surrounding areas. After prolonged talks with staff, it was agreed the depot should stay open but in a much slimmed down state. In fact half of the building was leased to Kent Engineering who actually needed larger premises. Other operations were transferred to Herne Bay, which had itself been given a reprieve from closure after the Market Analysis Project.

By 1984 it was clear the government had tired of running loss making nationalised industries – which demanded millions of pounds worth of subsidies – and was keen to return the businesses to the private sector. It duly published a White Paper clearing the way for total deregulation of the bus industry.

The document questioned the role of the NBC stating: "There is no good reason why local bus services should be provided by a national corporation."

The government was flushed by the success of privatising, among others, British Telecom and also the National Freight Corporation, the latter having been sold to its management and staff.

The die was cast and the return to private hands was a foregone conclusion. It was only a matter of how the industry should be sold off, not when or if. Initially, NBC bosses pressed for the organisation to be sold as one large going concern. Privately, East Kent managers, like other operators involved, were hoping the sale would centre around being offered as separate entities. The argument for this move was that it would create greater competition.

The white paper became law and the Transport Act of 1985 allowed for, among other things, the reorganisation of NBC into autonomous units to

132. There can be little doubt this AEC Regent V would have been written off after meeting an unexpectedly low bridge. Near the end of its useful life anyway, it languishes at Dover depot.

133. Dover's AEC Swift YJG 582K gets ready to depart Folkestone bus station bound for Hythe in 1983.

be sold off. By this time plans were well advanced in anticipation of this deregulation and much of the day to day management of East Kent was transferred to five district offices.

The Act required operators to register the journeys which it planned to run from October 1986 once privatisation took effect. Examination of East Kent's area revealed at this time, perhaps not surprisingly, that inter urban services made money while those in rural areas did not. Town services though varied from just breaking even to making heavy losses. Most evening and Sunday services ran at a loss while peak journeys varied depending on the length of the route and the resources committed to it.

New route patterns were settled as a result. Frequencies being increased around the Canterbury, Herne Bay and Whitstable area and on the main Thanet routes as well. Elsewhere, services were reduced in length, not only to have a chance of becoming profitable but enabling one district to have full control of the route.

East Kent's privatisation plans were given an important boost during the summer of 1986 when it successfully tendered from Kent County Council a series of routes, winning more than 90 per cent of the bids. So it was that the British bus industry, and East Kent with it, began a new era on Sunday 26 October 1986.

134. Discovered in the Chief Engineer's office when Kirby's Lane works closed was a Swiss made eight day Zenith clock. It was the master time piece by which all East Kent clocks would be set. Carried in a tamper proof outer box, the clock would be sent on a daily round to ensure clocks were synchronised.

135. Bristol VRTs with Eastern Coach Works bodies became the mainstay of the East Kent fleet in the late 1970s and early 1980s. A pair of them, in the new privatised livery, lay over at Folkestone bus station.

Back in private ownership

PERHAPS the most outwardly obvious sign to passengers that something had changed was the arrival on the area's roads of 45 yellow painted minibuses.

They served four different networks immediately from deregulation day covering Dover, Folkestone, Ashford and Canterbury. The chassis were 27 Ford Transits and 18 Freight Rover Sherpas, all equipped with 16 seater bodies by Folkestone based Dormobile – East Kent had been keen to keep business locally.

136. About to leave Dover is one of the many EK Minilink liveried Iveco minibuses. This one arrived from Brighton & Hove in 1990.

The vehicles were the first to be purchased in any great quantity by East Kent for a number of years. At the end of the 1970s there were still five small buses in the fleet.

Used on what were christened EK Minilink services, the vehicles were quite eyecatching in their yellow livery, finished with black and red waistbands.

Management realised before the minibuses took to the roads they would have to create new traffic, not merely take passengers from existing services, and ensure those driving them were properly at ease with the public. There were plenty of volunteers from within the company for the new jobs but the majority were recruited from outside, those with retail experience proving particularly popular. For this reason a number of lady drivers were hired, boosting their numbers considerably for the first time in years.

The Minilink concept was eagerly seized upon by passengers. More used to waiting a considerable time between double deckers, the idea of a smaller vehicle arriving every few minutes was welcomed with open arms.

More minibuses were soon ordered as their popularity continued and by early 1990 no fewer than a total of 86 were plying for trade in east

137. A row of double deckers parked up at the end of the day's work at The Garth, Canterbury, an open area on the opposite side of the road to St Stephen's garage.

Kent. Thanet had introduced a Minilink service in 1988 and others arrived in Herne Bay in 1990. Mainly 23 seaters by now, they covered one third of the company's route mileage.

No sooner had East Kent been deregulated than the senior managers were keen to buy it for themselves. Having gained the appropriate financial backing, they began negotiations with the NBC sales team in October 1986. Judging by the delays in talks, NBC must have been hoping for a better offer and one duly appeared from a French operator. This caused some concern for the home team as the price crept upwards. The management successfully sought additional financial help from merchant bankers Hill Samuel and eventually the company was sold by sealed bid. The sale was completed at London's Victoria Coach Station on 5 March 1987, East Kent being the 28th of 75 former NBC subsidiaries to return to the private sector.

Shortly after, the NBC arrow logo made way for the new EK scheme and buses appeared on the roads in a revised version of the traditional cherry and cream livery. It would take two years though before the NBC poppy red paintwork completely disappeared.

Although it wasn't a cash rich business, East Kent decided upon a programme of vehicle replacement, deciding its money was best spent on building a fleet mainly composed of

138. A small batch of two door Leyland Nationals were purchased from London Country in 1984. A number of them worked in Sealink livery to and from Dover docks.

minibuses and large capacity double deckers. Accordingly, 12 Atlanteans with Park Royal bodies were purchased second hand from Northern General in 1986.

Later on, the company decided upon a deal with MCW to purchase two new Hi-Liner coaches and 10 Metrobus double deckers as well as buying outright the five Metroliner coaches whose contract hire was nearing the end.

The double deckers arrived in 1988 and were the first new ones for nearly seven years. These were supplemented by 16 second hand Atlanteans from Greater Manchester Buses.

The new Metrobuses proved their worth and were specially noted for their efficient heating systems. A dozen more were put on order for arrival in 1989, seven being 70 seat capacity vehicles fitted with semi coach seats for long distance private hire work at weekends and school holidays.

The company acquired the coach holding of Marinair Travel in the late 1980s and this in turn became a subsidiary of East Kent, bringing with it a Mercedes minibus – sold to M&D in short order – and 12 Bova Europa and Futura coaches. A fall off in work though for these vehicles meant that by 1990 nine had been sold on to other operators.

Undeterred by the experience with these coaches, it was decided there was a market, albeit limited, for similar vehicles on excursion, tour and private hire uses and so four Metroliners were bought from Premier Travel. These came equipped with toilets and drinks machines. By adding an ex MCW demonstrator, East Kent suddenly had the country's largest fleet of single deck MCWs.

Contract coach work carried out for Shearings Holidays – formerly National Holidays – had reduced from requiring a dozen vehicles in the early eighties to just three by 1990 when it ceased altogether. Work for National Express proved more fruitful at this time though with 10 vehicles allocated to servicing its duties. National then came up with the idea in 1989 of using a standard vehicle rented to contractors. East Kent duly signed up for eight Volvo B10M coaches with Plaxton 3500 bodies that September for use between Kent and London.

139. This was one of 12 vehicles originally owned by Marinair Travel, taken over by East Kent in the late 1980s. Not only was this Bova example reliveried, it was re-registered with a 1959 origin Puffin number.

140. One of 10 85 seater Leyland Olympians rests at Canterbury alongside two older ECW bodied Bristol VRTs.

Two double deckers were written off and a third seriously damaged during a fire at Dover bus park in Pencester Road in April 1989. Two Scania replacements were ordered with 80 seat Alexander bodies and, for a brief time, were the largest buses in the fleet until surpassed the following year by delivery of 10 Leyland Olympians which could seat 85. These were built on long wheelbase chassis and carried Northern Counties bodywork.

141. The Central works in Canterbury and adjoining offices had been boarded up for sometime when this photograph was taken in 1993. Later on it would form part of a housing development called Carriage Mews.

1991 saw East Kent's 75th anniversary duly celebrated with a commemorative book and poster while scale models were made in limited numbers of some of the different types of vehicle it had operated down the years.

The company looked forward to more healthy times ahead, noting that over 20 million passengers had been carried in 1990 while a growing number of its staff had become shareholders.

East Kent was continuing to build up business and goodwill when in summer 1993 it was taken over by fast growing multi-national operator Stagecoach Group.

This organisation was formed in Scotland in 1980 by Ann Gloag and her brother Brian Souter, initially running express coach services from north of the border to London. By the time East Kent was acquired it had established itself as a major player in the industry and already owned other major names including Ribble, Bluebird Buses and United Counties. East Kent's near neighbour Southdown had joined the Stagecoach empire in 1989. As a result, rules governing competition and monopolies would have prevented Stagecoach from making a bid for Maidstone & District.

In 1993 Stagecoach employed 11,500 people in different parts of the world and ran 3,300 vehicles and it had just offered its shares on the Stock Exchange for the first time. Annual profits were running at nearly £13 million.

Stagecoach East Kent, as the new acquisition became known, would be managed from Lewes in East Sussex by the same team looking after Stagecoach South – the merged operations of the former Southdown, Hants & Surrey, Hampshire Bus, Coastline and South Coast Bus companies.

While commercial and operational control would continue to be run at local level, senior management at head office in Canterbury were surplus to requirements.

142. A 1988 Metrobus double decker was repainted into traditional East Kent cherry and cream to mark the company's 75th anniversary. Some proudly served customers climb aboard bound for Whitfield near Dover.

143. A later example of a Leyland Olympian, which arrived just after the Stagecoach takeover, picks up in Pencester Road, Dover, in 1994.

Ruthlessly and gracelessly, more than 30 managers at North Lane were given only a few minutes warning of their redundancy and told to clear their desks immediately – at least one career of over 25 years standing came to a sudden conclusion in this unhappy fashion.

Anybody wanting to drown their sorrows would have also found that social clubs in Canterbury, Thanet, Ashford and Folkestone depots were swiftly closed for good with the introduction of a no alcohol policy.

At the point of takeover East Kent employed 756 people and ran a fleet of 243 vehicles – considerably lower on both counts compared to the heydays of 40 years before and graphically showing the effects of society's shifts to not one but, often, two car ownership. By this time Thanet had lost its edge to being the largest area of East Kent. Thanks to reorganisation after privatisation, that mantle was held by Dover and Folkestone area which employed 277 people and 85 buses.

Coach holiday operations which had been revived by East Kent in the late 1980s – it published its own mini breaks brochures for home and abroad once more – were soon sold off by Stagecoach.

If Stagecoach had hoped to endear itself to its latest customers, then the initiative was perhaps lost amid allegations on BBCs Panorama in 1996 of forcing a competitor off the road. Thanet Bus, a small operator covering Ramsgate, Margate and Broadstairs, claimed its fares were being continually undercut by Stagecoach to take away its passengers. Although cast as villains of the piece, it emerged later that Stagecoach was only acting to protect its established business and claimed Thanet Bus was stealing its traffic rather than creating new business for itself.

In the late 1990s the new parent made sweeping changes as it integrated East Kent into the family. It took advantage of a rising property market, selling off two sites for redevelopment which were surplus to requirements. Part of the large apron of the Westwood garage in Ramsgate became the new home for a Ford dealership and a cut price supermarket.

In Ashford, the company retreated to the new garage at Cobbs Wood which had been built in 1976 and the town centre was disposed of.

In Canterbury, offices in North Lane were redeveloped into private apartments, the Central works and St Stephen's garage had been disposed of before Stagecoach's arrival.

144. Kirby's Lane, Canterbury, where the Central works was located until closure by Kent Engineering in 1985, is now a modern housing development.

Coincidentally, it was at this period of time that the old works gave way to housing.

In the late 1990s Herne Bay depot was destined to be sold off for demolition and development into another large supermarket. Failure to win planning permission and a need to store a greater number of buses, transferred from Canterbury, mean the site is still thriving as we write – despite occasional rumours to the contrary.

It would be wrong to cast Stagecoach in the guise of an asset stripper. Considerable investments have been made in new vehicles and the network infrastructure in recent years. After takeover, many of the older buses were

145. Barton Mill Court stands on the site previously occupied by the St Stephen's garage in Canterbury.

146. Despite rumours to the contrary, Herne Bay depot continues to operate and houses many of the Canterbury and Whitstable area vehicles.

sold on, particularly the last of the ageing and now unpopular Leyland Nationals. Often the replacements included newer – but not new – Leyland Titans and Scanias, transferred from Stagecoach operations in London.

Stagecoach lost little time introducing its white bodied with arrow headed stripes livery to the area. East Kent vehicles being retained were resprayed once again, some wearing their third set of colours in less than 10 years.

147. The former headquarters building in Station Road West, Canterbury, was converted into apartments during the late 1990s.

148. A Kent Clipper liveried vehicle arrives at Canterbury from Folkestone. Like the Compass service, Clipper suffered from meeting too many traffic hold ups on its lengthy route and is now three separate services.

As one would expect from a company of its size, Stagecoach was, and still is, a major purchaser of new vehicles in the UK. When it took over East Kent it was buying 300 buses a year. As it introduced new ones to high usage inner cities, so existing vehicles were moved on to replace older ones in other areas. By the mid 1990s the average age of a Stagecoach bus was eight years – and falling. The job of moving vehicles around was made easier for having a standard corporate livery which only required the name of the operating company to be replaced. Thus a South Coast bus would, after swapping a couple of pieces of vinyl, soon become an East Kent one.

At the same time, digital destination displays

149. Work had already started on improving Canterbury bus station when this photo was taken. Note the temporary railings around vehicles to direct the public to the vehicle entrance. A new office building has been completed back left.

150. One of the first buses to operate the Canterbury Park & Ride scheme was a grey painted Northern Counties bodied Leyland Olympian. Here, it is back on stage duties working between the city and Faversham.

were making their first appearance. Until now, it had been the job of the conductor, and later one man operator, to wind blinds manually to tell passengers where their bus was headed. This called for some precision to ensure the right parts of the blinds were clearly on show. No such guesswork with a digital version, just a matter of keying in the right code to the display's computer module.

If a subsidiary wanted brand new vehicles, it had to make a powerful business case to senior management at HQ in Scotland and this was achieved by East Kent towards the turn of the century when Park & Ride buses, single and double decker, were acquired for use in an ongoing contract with Canterbury City Council. More highly specified in passenger comfort than other new buses, these metallic grey painted vehicles were designed to make a favourable impression of bus travel on their usually car driving passengers. It's a fair bet that travelling Park & Ride is the only time many car users go anywhere by bus!

Making bus travel attractive and a viable alternative to the car has been an ongoing challenge for East Kent and the industry as a whole for decades. Even in the mid 1960s the company's staff magazine Omnibus was quoting Ernest Marples, the then Minister of Transport, at some length on the need for good quality public transport to avoid complete log jam.

It wasn't until the late 1990s that any real efforts to win over car owners appeared to be made – Canterbury's Park & Ride being a good local example.

Another initiative was the Compass network. This was a circular service linking all the main towns in East Kent with buses taking clockwise or anti-clockwise routes around the area. A good concept, it ultimately failed owing to increasing traffic congestion in some areas which meant punctuality became unpredictable. Managers realised buses were hitting one traffic hold up after another as progress became increasingly slower.

Since then low floor buses – which see the body rising and falling at a specially heightened bus stop – have taken to the roads and now make up a significant proportion of East Kent's current fleet. Elderly and disabled people and parents with pushchairs have benefited from this measure to ease access on and off buses – a far cry from a conductor helping a mum with her pushchair off a rear platform.

Innovation has not been limited to the vehicles. On the busiest routes in the area Kent County Council has invested in displays telling passengers how many minutes they can expect to wait for the next bus to show up at that particular stop. A real blessing for people more

151. *Demolishing the 1950s office building at Canterbury. The clock had long gone and had been replaced by a piece of black painted timber.*

accustomed to making a guess at when a bus is likely to arrive.

During 2002 Canterbury bus station was given a comprehensive makeover in tandem with the nearby multi-million pound Whitefriars redevelopment scheme. The 1950s office building was demolished with neighbouring small shops to make way for an entirely new arrangement.

Buses now park front on into angled bays set out along the length of the station, facing the retail development itself. Again, digital displays are much in evidence flagging arrivals and departures. A strikingly designed circular travel office stands over the site of the old one while new offices and staff canteen have been built at the far end closest to the former Riding Gate.

152. *A Herne Bay based Dennis Trident makes a rare sortie to Folkestone to join in the celebrations marking the 50th anniversary of that town's bus station in Bouverie Square. An Optare Solo pulls in alongside.*

153. A total of 21 women drivers were based at Westwood depot in 2004. Thirteen of the 'Stagecoach Angels' pose during the launch of the Thanet Loop service in September of that year.

154. You can wait ages for a bus and then 17 turn up! All of the Canterbury Triangle vehicles parade along one of the bus lanes beside the city wall soon after arrival in September 2004.

During 2004, the Bouverie Square terminus in Folkestone received the facelift treatment largely funded by Shepway District Council. New light, airy, vandal resistant metal and toughened glass shelters structures, complete with rotating advertising posters and digital displays were installed while offices were repainted.

Celebration of the terminus' 50th anniversary was marked over the Easter holiday in March 2005 with a bus rally involving a number of preserved vehicles of the types which had been a common sight there in the past.

The town's 35 strong fleet had been reinforced in the previous October with nine Optare Solo buses, costing a total of just over £600,000. Capable of carrying 27 seated passengers, these vehicles have a ramp that bridges the gap between the kerb and the entrance and have large, low, flat

155. Alastair Darling, Secretary of State for Transport, second from right, joins local dignitaries in launching the Thanet Loop service at Westwood depot in Thanet.

floor areas enabling wheelchair users and parents with push chairs to get on and off easily.

September 2004 saw the launch of the Canterbury Triangle service with the arrival of 17 new low floor, easy access Alexander bodied Dennis Trident double decker buses.

Costing £2.5 million, the scheme represented the first phase of a series of bus improvements planned by the partners of the Canterbury Quality Bus Partnership, Stagecoach, Kent County Council and Canterbury City Council.

The Triangle provides an every 15 minute service between Canterbury, Whitstable and Herne Bay using the specially liveried Tridents.

On October, Thanet took delivery of £1.6 million worth of 18 new Alexander bodied Dennis Darts providing a service every 10 minutes between Ramsgate, Margate and Broadstairs known as the Thanet Loop. Early indications showed the service carrying more customers than anticipated.

Secretary of State for Transport Alastair Darling cut a banner at Westwood depot to launch the Loop which had been jointly funded as a Kickstart initiative between the government and the Stagecoach Group. This was supplemented by more than £550,000 from Government Urban Bus Challenge and Kent County Council local transport funding.

156. Transport Minister and Thanet South MP Steve Ladyman cuts a celebratory cake with dignitaries and Stagecoach officials at the newly opened Westwood Cross for the unveiling of the Thanet Stars service.

Such was the success of the Loop service with passengers, that in June 2005 Stagecoach invested another £600,000 for nine more Optare Solos to launch its Thanet Stars service. They provided links between different areas of Margate and Ramsgate with the Westwood Cross shopping centre which had opened earlier in the month.

This latest clutch of Solos was among the first to be delivered in a nationwide programme by Stagecoach to coax more motorists out of their cars. All told, the Solos were part of a 340 vehicle order for mini, midi and double decker buses scheduled to take to the roads with provincial subsidiaries between June 2005 and February 2006.

Clearly, if the bus is to remain viable, more motorists need to feel they can leave their cars behind and use a service which can balance the factors of fast, frequent, reliable and cheap.

There's plenty of work still to do in coming anywhere near achieving these aims but with the right political will and investment in vehicles and network, the scene would be set for success.

157. Poster circa 1950.

EXPRESS COACH SERVICES

KENT COAST

LONDON

EAST KENT
EXPRESS COACHES

DAILY SERVICES AT CHEAP FARES
ASK FOR LEAFLET AT ANY
EAST KENT OFFICE OR AGENCY

158. Poster circa 1963.

159. Poster circa 1957.

HIRE A COACH

FOR THE BIG OCCASION

DAY EXCURSIONS

TATTOOS & TOURNAMENTS

SPORTING EVENTS

DANCE & THEATRE PARTIES

PRIVATE

EAST KENT

EAST KENT

Your local "EAST KENT" office or agent will be pleased to help with quotations, bookings and itineraries

160. Poster circa 1959.

Photographic credits and bibliography

The author is indebted to the following for their kind permission in allowing photographs and artefacts to be included in this book:

Maidstone & District and East Kent Bus Club for use of photographs numbered 1, 4, 5, 6, 8, 9, 11, 12, 15, 16, 17, 22, 23, 24, 27, 28, 29, 32, 34, 37, 38, 39, 40, 43, 45, 48, 49, 50, 51, 52, 56, 57, 61, 62, 64, 65, 69, 70, 83, 85, 87, 88, 89, 109, 110, 111, 112, 115, 116 and 138

Mr Ian Robertson for use of photographs and artefacts numbered 7, 10, 18, 19, 30, 31, 32, 33, 41, 42, 44, 46, 60, 63, 84, 92, 93, 96, 98, 102, 103, 104, 105, 106, 107, 108, 114, 120, 125, 128 and 129

Mr David Ferguson for use of photographs numbered 117, 123, 131, 132, 133, 135, 136, 137, 139, 140, 141, 142, 143, 148, 149 and 150

Mr Paul Crampton for use of photographs numbered 77, 78, 79, 80, 81, 82, 90, 91, 97, 99 and 151

Stagecoach East Kent for use of photographs and artefacts numbered 54, 152, 153, 154, 155, 156, 157, 158, 159 and 160

Margate Museum, Margate, for use of photographs numbered 59, 68, 86, 94 and 95

Mr Eammonn Kentell for use of photographs numbered 119, 121, 122, 124 and 130

Mr Colin Smith for use of artefacts featured in photographs numbered 55, 72, 113 and 134

Dover Transport Museum for use of photographs numbered 74 and 75

The Kentish Gazette newspaper, Canterbury (Kent Messenger Group) for use of photographs numbered 26 and 35

Mr Mike Ansell for use of photograph number 66

All other photographs are from the author's collection

We've been careful to ensure photographs are credited to the right sources but any issues arising may be addressed to the author.

Bibliography: ABC of East Kent by S Poole, published by Ian Allan 1948
East Kent Road Car Company Jubilee 1916-1966 published by East Kent 1966
East Kent – An Illustrated Fleet History, 1916-1978 published by M&D and EK Bus Club 1978
East Kent by Frank Woodworth published by Capital Transport 1991
Glory Days of East Kent by Glyn Kraemer-Johnson & John Bishop published by Ian Allan 2005